MARCHENA
(Bindloe)

TOWER (Genovesa)

Darwin Bay

HOLOMEW

idge Rocks

SEYMOUR (N. Seymour)

APHNE

BALTRA (S. Seymour)

SANTA CRUZ
(Indefatigable)

Bellavista

PLAZA

Academy Bay

Tortuga Bay

BARRINGTON
(Santa Fe)

Kicker Rock

Pta. &
Isla
Pitt

SAN CRISTOBAL
(Chatham)

Wreck Bay

OW

CHAMPION

nt

ENDERBY

CALDWELL

GARDNER

WATSON

aria)

Gardner Bay

Pta. Cevallos

HOOD (Española)

THE COLLINS FIELD GUIDE TO THE
BIRDS OF GALAPAGOS

THE COLLINS FIELD GUIDE TO THE

Birds of Galapagos

Michael Harris

*with 12 plates
and 68 line illustrations by*

BARRY KENT MACKAY

THE STEPHEN GREENE PRESS

Lexington, Massachusetts

COLLINS FIELD GUIDE TO THE BIRDS OF GALAPAGOS

THE STEPHEN GREENE PRESS, INC.

Published by the Penguin Group
Viking Penguin Inc., 40 West 23rd Street, New York,
New York 10010, U.S.A.
Penguin Books Ltd, 27 Wrights Lane, London W8 5TZ, England
Penguin Books Australia Ltd, Ringwood, Victoria, Australia
Penguin Books Canada Ltd, 2801 John Street, Markham, Ontario,
Canada L3R 1B4
Penguin Books (N.Z.) Ltd, 182-190 Wairau Road, Auckland 10,
New Zealand

Penguin Books Ltd, Registered Offices: Harmondsworth, Middlesex,
England

First published in Great Britain in 1974 under the title
A FIELD GUIDE TO THE BIRDS OF GALAPAGOS
by William Collins Sons & Co., Ltd.
Revised edition published in 1982
First published in the United States of America in 1989
by The Stephen Greene Press, Inc.
Distributed by Viking Penguin Inc.

10 9 8 7 6 5 4 3 2 1   1 3 5 7 9 10 8 6 4 2   1 2 3 4 5 6 7 8 9 10

CIP data available

Printed in Hong Kong
by South China Printing Co.
Set in Times

Contents

Plates

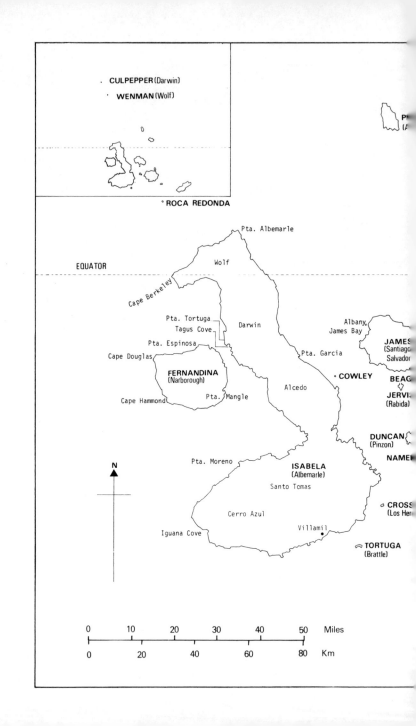

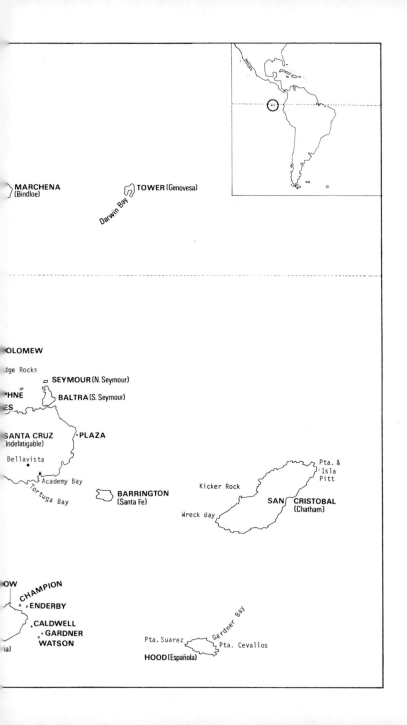

Preface

Although for more than a century the Galapagos have been numbered among the most famous of archipelagos, it is only recently that it has become possible for the ordinary person to visit the islands without sacrificing a great deal of time and suffering not inconsiderable discomforts. Most visitors to the islands are already attracted by the birds, or rapidly become so. Much has been written concerning the birds of the area, but it is mostly in scientific periodicals and often of rather a dry nature. Up to now the only way to identify many Galapagos species has been by comparison with named skin collections - a rather unsatisfactory situation to say the least. The present volume is an attempt to fill the need for a useful field guide to the birds of these islands.

Unlike many other books covering large and very diverse faunistic areas, we are here concerned with relatively few bird species, but species which have been very important in the understanding of both the evolution and ecology of birds. Therefore it has seemed desirable to include some general information on the birds - which, it is hoped, will answer some of the questions asked by visitors to the islands. Galapagos birds are mostly both common and tame, so it is usually possible to see and comprehend many of the points raised in these sections.

Introduction

How to use the species accounts

NOMENCLATURE

As species are always evolving, it is sometimes very difficult to define the distinctions between one species and a closely related one. The classic criterion, whether or not the two supposed species will interbreed to produce fertile offspring, is of little use if the species do not meet in the wild. Island birds are important in demonstrating evolution, for a single species colonising an archipelago will often give rise to different forms or even species on different islands. However, these inter-island differences pose difficulties as to whether or not the species now found is the same as that extant on the nearby continental land mass, and to whether the populations on the different islands should be considered distinct species or mere subspecies. It is essential that we can name the birds we are dealing with, so many arbitrary decisions must be made. In most cases I have followed Swarth's (1931) designation of the species found in Galapagos, modified in a few cases by more recent work — most especially that of Lack (1945) on the finches. A few species have been moved from their normally accepted systematic position to be next to similar-looking species in order to facilitate comparisons.

IDENTIFICATION

Many species will be identified from the plates but reference should also be made to the relevant species descriptions.

Although the size of a bird is often critical for identification it is very difficult to describe in a meaningful way. The length of the bird (designated 1.) from bill tip to tail is given, also the wing spread (w.s.) and length of bill (b.) if these are important. Flight is only described if it is a useful aid to identification.

Most migrant birds are only seen in their nonbreeding plumages but occasionally birds will remain in the islands during the northern summer and even attain breeding attire. If such plumages have been recorded in the area, they are given, if they have yet to be seen but could conceivably occur, they are given in brackets. If you have any doubt as to some seemingly peculiar plumage, especially of waders, you are referred to one of the excellent North American Field Guides because several other species, e.g. Long-billed Dowitcher, might occur in the future. Unusual seabirds should be compared with the plates and descriptions in Tuck's 'Field Guide to the Seabirds of Britain and the World.'

VOICE

An attempt is made to render the commonest calls of most species but in only a few instances is it possible to identify any of the resident birds by sound alone. Beware of inter-island differences in bird songs.

FOOD AND BREEDING

Basic information concerning the Galapagos populations where such data are available. Age of first breeding is the youngest ringed bird found with an egg or young. Most birds do not breed until a year or more older.

DISTRIBUTION

A brief statement of the status of the species, its range within the islands and where likely to be seen. Also given is the range of the species outside the islands: in migrants this is restricted to movements within the Americas.

Great care must be taken in the identification of landbirds on islands where they are not know to occur. Consideration must be given to the possibility of freak individuals and hybrids.

List of birds of Galapagos

*Galapagos Penguin
 Waved Albatross
 Hawaiian (Dark-rumped) Petrel
 Audubon's Shearwater
 White-vented (Elliot's) Storm
  Petrel
 Band-rumped (Madeiran) Storm
  Petrel
 Wedge-rumped (Galapagos)
  Storm Petrel
 Red-billed Tropicbird
 Brown Pelican
 Blue-footed Booby
 Masked (White) Booby
 Red-footed Booby
*Flightless Cormorant
 Great Frigatebird
 Magnificent Frigatebird
 Great Blue Heron
 Common Egret
*Lava Heron
 Striated Heron
 Yellow-crowned Night Heron
 Greater Flamingo
 White-cheeked Pintail
*Galapagos Hawk
*Galapagos Rail
 Paint-billed Crake
 Common Gallinule
 Oystercatcher

 Common Stilt
 Swallow-tailed Gull
*Lava Gull
 Sooty Tern
 Brown Noddy
*Galapagos Dove
 Dark-billed Cuckoo
 Barn Owl
 Short-eared Owl
 Vermilion Flycatcher
*Large-billed Flycatcher
*Galapagos Martin
*Galapagos Mockingbird
*Charles Mockingbird
*Hood Mockingbird
*Chatham Mockingbird
 Yellow Warbler
*Small Ground Finch
*Medium Ground Finch
*Large Ground Finch
*Sharp-beaked Ground Finch
*Cactus Finch
*Large Cactus Finch
*Vegetarian Finch
*Small Tree Finch
*Medium Tree Finch
*Large Tree Finch
*Woodpecker Finch
*Mangrove Finch
*Warbler Finch

REGULAR MIGRANTS († Species most likely to be seen)

Cape Pigeon
Sooty Shearwater
Snowy Egret
Cattle Egret
Blue-winged Teal
Osprey
Peregrine
†Semipalmated Plover
†Black-bellied (Grey) Plover
†Ruddy Turnstone
Solitary Sandpiper
Lesser Yelowlegs
Greater Yellowlegs
†Spotted Sandpiper
†Wandering Tattler
Willet

Western Sandpiper
†Least Sandpiper
†Sanderling
†Whimbrel
Short-billed Dowitcher
†Northern (Red-necked)
' Phalarope
†Wilson's Phalarope
†Franklin's Gull
Royal Tern
Common Tern
Belted Kingfisher
Purple Martin
Bank Swallow (Sand Martin)
Barn Swallow
Bobolink

ACCIDENTALS (‡ = May be regular in extremely small numbers)

Pied-billed Grebe
Wandering or Royal Albatross
Black-footed Albatross
Giant Petrel
Black Petrel
Flesh-footed Shearwater
Wedge-tailed Shearwater
Dove Prion
White-faced Storm Petrel
White-bellied Storm Petrel
‡Leach's Storm Petrel
Markham's Storm Petrel
Black Storm Petrel
Brown Booby
Black-crowned Night Heron
Black-bellied Tree Duck
Purple Gallinule
Sora Rail
Golden Plover
Thick-billed Plover
Killdeer
Black Turnstone
‡Surfbird
Knot

‡Semipalmated Sandpiper
‡Baird's Sandpiper
White-rumped Sandpiper
Pectoral Sandpiper
Stilt Sandpiper
‡Marbled Godwit
Hudsonian Godwit
‡Red (Grey) Phalarope
Southern or South Polar Skua
Pomarine Jaeger
Parasitic Jaeger
Long-tailed Jaeger
‡Laughing Gull
Southern Black-backed (Kelp) Gull
Black Tern
Fairy Tern
Eared Dove
Black-billed Cuckoo
Groove-billed Ani
Smooth-billed Ani
Common Nighthawk
Chimney Swift
Cliff Swallow
Summer Tanager

History of ornithology in Galapagos

Ornithology in Galapagos can be taken as having started in 1835 with the visit of Charles Darwin on H.M.S. *Beagle.* Darwin's accounts of his travels and discoveries sparked off considerable interest in the avifauna and tortoises, and several major expeditions were mounted to the archipelago. These are listed chronologically below, along with endemic birds which were collected for the first time by that expedition.

1835 Visit of Charles Darwin on H.M.S. *Beagle.* The birds collected were described by Gould and contained eight species of Darwin's Finches, Galapagos Hawk, Galapagos Dove, Galapagos Rail, Charles, Galapagos and Chatham Mockingbirds and Large-billed Flycatcher.

1839 The French Frigate *Venus* brought back the first Swallow-tailed Gull and Galapagos Martin.

1852 Dr Kinberg on the Swedish frigate *Eugenie* collected the Lava Heron and Galapagos Penguin.

1868 Large collections made by S. Habel and described by Salvin contained the Sharp-beaked Ground Finch and Woodpecker Finch.

1888 Visits by U.S.F.S. *Albatross.* Collections included Hood Mocking-
& 91 bird, Large Cactus Finch and Medium Tree Finch.

1897 Over 3,000 skins collected by the Webster-Harris Expedition on the schooner *Lila and Mattie.* Described by Rothschild and Hartert. The discovery of the Flightless Cormorant and the nesting area of the Waved Albatross.

1898 The visit of the Heller-Snodgrass Expedition of the Stanford Uni-
-99 versity aboard the sealing schooner *Julia E. Whalen.* Mangrove Finch.

1905 By far the most thorough survey of the fauna and flora yet made was
-06 undertaken by the expedition of the California Academy of Sciences aboard the schooner *Academy.* 5,800 bird skins were collected and worked on by Swarth.

This was the last of the major collecting expeditions but by this time a vast quantity of skins were residing in the museums of the world. In 1938-9 David Lack and L. S. V. Venables did field work on the landbirds, the former worker producing his now-classic monograph on the finches. Since this date various field workers, especially I and L. K. Abbott, P. D. Boersma, R. I. Bowman, A. Brosset, M. Castro, E. Curio, J. F. Downhower, P. R. Grant, J. P. Hailman, M. P. Harris, P. Kramer, R. Lévêque, J. B. Nelson, J. N. M. Smith, D. W. and B. K. Snow, T. de Vries, have made large contributions to our knowledge of the ornithology.

With the great increase in the numbers of visitors to Galapagos it is inevitable that species will be added to the islands' list and the status of the migrant species will need redefining. The author would welcome any records of new or rare species (with descriptions please). They should be sent to him at:—

THE INSTITUTE OF TERRESTRIAL ECOLOGY
Hill of Brathens
Banchory
Kincardineshire AB3 4BY
Scotland

Climate

Despite their equatorial situation, the islands are surrounded by relatively cold waters brought northwards by the Humboldt Current. The overall climate is probably best designated as subtropical but varies greatly from season to season, and year to year, due to changes in the strength and limits of the current.

There are two rather distinct seasons known as 'warm' and 'cold'. (Sometimes the terms 'wet' and 'dry' are used but these are very ambiguous, meaning entirely different things when applied to the coastal and upland areas. The 'dry' season often has more precipitation than the 'wet' — so these two terms are best forgotten.)

During the warm season, which lasts from January to April, the Humboldt Current has relatively little influence on the islands and the sea temperatures are relatively high. Air temperatures may reach tropical levels, the skies are usually clear but sometimes large cumulus clouds gather and these may give heavy rains. Later in the year, the cool season, sea-temperatures drop as the northern edge of the Current moves past the islands, and the winds which, at least in the southern islands, are predominantly from the south-east are cooled. This leads to an inversion over the area, giving low stratiform clouds which persist for much of the day. These clouds give some slight precipitation in coastal areas but this is insufficient to allow plants to come into leaf. However, in the highlands there is considerable rain — often more than in the warm season. The drizzle which occurs at this time is known as *garua,* a name sometimes also applied to the season.

Rainfall is extremely erratic. On the coast annual rainfall can be less than 1″ or as much as 55″, inland the recorded extremes are 15″ and 80″. The extremely wet years are associated with 'failures' of the Humboldt Current which allow warm waters from farther north in the Gulf of Panama to flow south and surround the islands. This south-flowing current is the 'El Niño' and in extreme years may affect areas as far south as southern Peru and then there are large-scale mortalities among the guano birds in these areas. As yet there is no evidence of sea-bird mortalities in Galapagos which can be associated with this phenomenon, but breeding of some seabirds, such as Flightless Cormorant and Waved Albatross may be upset.

Six-year averages 1965-70 of meterological readings taken at Academy Bay, (Santa Cruz) by the Charles Darwin Research Station.

	J	F	M	A	M	J	J	A	S	O	N	D
Average Max. ° C	28.0	29.6	30.6	29.5	27.9	26.0	24.6	24.2	24.3	25.2	25.8	26.7
Average Min. ° C	22.8	23.2	22.7	22.7	22.1	21.1	19.8	19.1	19.1	19.6	20.4	20.9
Hours of sunshine	5.3	7.5	6.0	7.5	5.2	4.4	2.8	3.3	2.9	3.8	3.5	4.0
Rainfall (inches) at Academy Bay (sea level)	0.78	0.89	1.30	1.34	1.13	0.31	0.32	0.28	0.41	0.42	0.31	0.29
Rainfall (inches) at Bellavista (558′)	3.1	2.86	3.13	2.00	2.12	1.46	2.52	1.81	2.94	2.07	1.93	1.78
Sea temperature ° C	24.4	25.2	24.9	25.0	24.5	23.1	22.0	21.5	21.8	22.3	23.0	23.3

Zonation of plants and birds in relation to altitude

Although much of the land mass of Galapagos is low lying and covered with rather arid scrubland, most of the larger islands are high enough to have several distinct vegetation zones. Despite the marked inter-island differences in flora associated with differing climatic conditions, geological age and substrate, and degree of damage caused to the native plant communities by man, his animals and plants, there is a general pattern of zonation among the plants. The main zones and their birds are put forward below. For more details concerning plants the reader is referred to the account in Wiggins and Porter (1971), but it must be stressed that although the zonation is clear on some islands, e.g. Santa Cruz, on others, especially Floreana, it needs a trained botanist to sort things out.

Unlike plants, birds can change their habitats as conditions become especially favourable or unfavourable, so that in times of drought or unusual rains, species may appear in numbers where they do not normally nest. For instance on Santa Cruz the Warbler Finch is usually rare on the coast and ground finches uncommon high up, but rains allow the former to move to coastal areas, and sometimes even nest, and droughts are followed by large upward movements of Small and Medium Ground Finches. Other species, especially the Dark-billed Cuckoo, fluctuate widely in their numbers but it is unclear whether this is due to intra-island movements or overall population fluctuations.

The bird lists given below refer to islands which have several definite vegetation zones. The small islands with only an arid zone have rather peculiar avifaunas and these are discussed on pages 25-6. Birds marked* occur only in small numbers though they have their centre of distribution in this zone.

MANGROVE ZONE

This distinctive zone is restricted to very sheltered areas of coastline.

Common birds	*Present*	*Rare*
Herons	*Mangrove Finch	Woodpecker Finch
Yellow Warbler	(Isabela, Fernandina)	Vermilion Flycatcher
Small Ground Finch	Medium Ground Finch	
Mockingbird	Dark-billed Cuckoo	

ARID COASTAL ZONE

This zone is typified by *Opuntia* cacti, spiny bushes and relatively small trees. Apart from some evergreen bushes and the sprawling *Cryptocarpus,* the plants of this area are mainly grey looking and leafless; only after heavy rains do the trees come into leaf or is there any growth of grasses or sedges. Even this greenery is short-lived as a few weeks of sun are sufficient to burn off most of the annual plants. In a few areas there are open stands of *Bursera* — reminiscent of English parkland. This zone does not get enough moisture from the garua of the cold season to become green.

Common birds	*Present*	*Rare*
Small Ground Finch	*Large Ground Finch	Vermilion Flycatcher
Medium Ground Finch	Vegetarian Finch	Warbler Finch
	Woodpecker Finch	Barn Owl
Cactus Finch	Small Tree Finch	
Yellow Warbler	Dark-billed Cuckoo	
Galapagos Dove	Short-eared Owl	
Mockingbird	Galapagos Martin	
	Large-billed Flycatcher	

TRANSITIONAL ZONE

At a slightly higher elevation, average 200 feet, the general impression of the vegetation changes; the cacti and trees become taller and rather closer together, there is a dense under-story of perennial plants (some of which manage to keep green throughout the year), and the hanging lichen *Ramalina* becomes common. Many of the shrubs are evergreen and a few ferns and epiphytic plants manage to exist in protected locations. In the higher parts of the zone cacti become scarce and eventually disappear.

Common birds	*Present*	*Rare*
Small Ground Finch	Large Ground Finch	Large Tree Finch
Medium Ground Finch	Large-billed Flycatcher	Galapagos Martin
	Dark-billed Cuckoo	
Vegetarian Finch	Vermilion Flycatcher	
Cactus Finch	Warbler Finch	
(lower part)	Woodpecker Finch	
Small Tree Finch	Barn Owl	
Mockingbird	Short-eared Owl	
Yellow Warbler		
Galapagos Dove		

HUMID ZONE

This term is used for an area of dense vegetation where there are normally two rainy periods a year. There are two easily recognisable subdivisions. The first is the Scalesia zone. Scalesia is a tree composite which does occur lower down but here it becomes dominant. Although sometimes open with quantities of ground vegetation including many vines, the canopy may be thick enough to prevent growth of ground vegetation. The trees may be clothed with epiphytes.

On Santa Cruz, and formerly to a lesser extent on San Cristóbal, an evergreen shrub *Miconia* forms almost impenetrable areas above 1,300 feet. The bushes themselves are coated with epiphytes and the more open areas are carpeted with normal and tree ferns, and sedges. For at least six months of the year the whole area is dripping with water. This zone is rapidly being cleared for cattle raising and this causes concern for the Hawaiian Petrel, which nests here.

Common birds	*Present*	*Rare*
Warbler Finch	Medium Ground Finch	Cactus Finch
Large Tree Finch	Small Ground Finch	
Medium Tree Finch	Mockingbird	
(Floreana)	*Paint-billed Crake	
Small Tree Finch	*Woodpecker Finch	
Sharp-beaked Ground	Barn Owl	
Finch (James, Pinta,		
Fernandina)		
Large-billed Flycatcher		
Vermilion Flycatcher		
Dark-billed Cuckoo		
Yellow Warbler		
Galapagos Rail		
Short-eared Owl		

FERN—SEDGE ZONE

Immediately above the tree zones is an area where the only large plants are tree ferns. Virtually all the plants are perennials — the commonest being sedges, mosses, club mosses, grasses and liverworts. In some area there are considerable areas of *Sphagnum* moss. This zone is the result of widespread grazing and man-made fires. Once there were probably many more plant species, and more tree ferns and isolated *Miconia* bushes.

Common birds	*Present*
Galapagos Rail	Medium Ground Finch (when dry)
Galapagos Martin	Small Ground Finch (when dry)
(few areas)	Yellow Warbler
	Short-eared Owl

On some of the volcanoes of Isabela, there is an even higher zone which is slightly drier and where some Prickly Pear cacti again appear. There are few observations of birds here but Cactus and ground finches, Galapagos Mockingbirds and Martins occur.

Numbers of landbirds, plants and altitude

From the previous discussion on the zonation of plants and birds, it is clear that the more vegetation zones on an island, the more bird species the island can support. A statistical analysis of the numbers of species of landbirds found breeding on the main islands in relation to the various physical and botanical characteristics of these islands, shows that three factors are important. These are the number of plant species, the altitude and the distance from an island to the next main island. Plants are by far the most important consideration but only up to a certain level — above that level an increase in the number of plant species does not bring about a further increase in the variety of landbirds present. The height of an island also exerts an influence even after account is taken for the fact that altitude itself is mainly, but not entirely, responsible for the number of plants on an island. Isolation (as expressed by the square of the distance to the next main island) brings about a decrease in the number of landbirds but this is relatively unimportant when compared to plants and altitude in influencing the avifauna.

THE LANDBIRDS OF ARID ISLANDS

As a general rule, the more diverse is a habitat, the more species of birds it can support. Several of the main islands, although relatively large, are low-lying so that they have only an arid vegetation zone and an associated small list of plant species. As anticipated these have fewer landbirds than the higher islands. The exceptions to the rule are low islands near to large islands and these rely to a considerable extent on recruitment of humid zone birds from these high islands. For this reason Seymour and Baltra are considered as part of Santa Cruz as far as the bird lists are concerned.

Birds such as the Vegetarian Finch which rely on green vegetation for their food cannot survive on these arid islands, neither can those which need a supply of large insects or caterpillars, e.g. the Dark-billed Cuckoo, the tree and Woodpecker finches. There are, however, enough small insects, as shown by the island-wide distribution of the Warbler Finch and Yellow Warbler. The Large-billed Flycatcher is adapted to living in the arid zone of many islands but even this bird is apparently unable to survive on Tower. But what of birds which feed on seeds? The Dove is widespread so must find sufficient of its small seeds almost everywhere; the Ground and Cactus finches, on the other hand, have a rather patchy distribution, but this can often be explained by a knowledge of their ecology.

Hood and Tower are low-lying islands with few flowering plants, 96 and 40 species respectively. The Large Cactus Finch is found on both islands, but there are two different forms, a large-billed subspecies on Hood, and a small-billed form on Tower. In addition Tower has the Large Ground Finch (with a very large beak) and the Sharp-beaked Ground Finch (small beak), and Hood the Small Ground Finch (small beak). The Sharp-beaked and Small Ground Finches are very similar and presumably compete for food as where both occur, they are in different vegetation zones. Observations on these islands suggest that the different bills enable species to deal efficiently with different seeds, and that on small islands these species eat a greater range of foods than they do on large islands. It is probably no coincidence that the Large Cactus Finch does not occur with the Medium Ground Finch or the Cactus Finch for its bill is intermediate between that of the two species. However it is likely that the Medium Ground Finch once was resident on Hood (14 specimens collected by Academy expedition) and this might be expected as Tower with less plant species has three seed-eating finches, whereas Hood now has only two. If the Medium Ground Finch was on Hood it would nicely fill the gap between the very large-billed Large Cactus Finch and the small-billed Small Ground Finch, and to some extent explain why the Hood Large Cactus Finch has evolved such a massive bill.

The smaller an area, the smaller the number of individual land birds it can support, but if the numbers are too small the species may become extinct by normal population fluctuations. The more specialised a species becomes, also the rarer it is, and so the greater chances of extinction. Small islands have a few rather generalised species, whereas larger islands allow a greater diversity of species to exist.

Breeding seasons

The majority of Galapagos birds are very tame even when breeding and all visitors will encounter some birds which have either eggs or young. This section gives a brief summary of our knowledge on the breeding seasons and the factors which are important in bringing about their timing. In recent years considerable attention has been paid to the breeding of the birds but future work will doubtless produce many records of out-of-season nesting. Sea-, water- (apart from sea) and land-birds are best treated separately but first a few words on why birds breed when they do will not be out of place.

The timing of breeding cycles in animals is influenced by two distinct sets of factors known as the ultimate and the proximate. The ultimate factor has been evolved by the birds nesting at the best time leaving the most offspring. Birds nesting at other times will raise few, if any, young and so the trait for breeding then will soon disappear from the population. Food, normally that available for feeding the young, is the most important ultimate factor. In most people's minds, spring and summer, rather than winter, are the times for birds' nests but in the tropics such distinctions lose their importance.

Proximate factors enable the birds to anticipate the best time for breeding. It is of little use for a species to be adapted to raising its young on a food which is only available in April, unless the individuals have some clue to guide them in laying eggs a month or so before this time. In many temperate birds the increasing day length is the main factor involved in this timing but availability of food may also be important. Even in the tropics there are very few places with a completely seasonless environment so that there are always some clues to tell birds when the breeding season is approaching.

SEABIRDS

To the casual observer the breeding of the seabirds in the archipelago is confusing but studies have shown several types of breeding cycle. The recorded egg dates and the intervals between layings in various species are given on page 29.

As mentioned earlier there are marked seasonal variations in the temperature of the sea due to the movements of the Humboldt Current, but there is no obvious associated variation in the plankton. It is conceivable that the sampling technique was inadequate but the fact that some seabirds breed at different times each year suggests that there is no seasonal fluctuation of overriding importance.

The overall pattern is of a uniform level of seabird breeding throughout the year but in no species is there a constant level of nesting in all months. Many of the species have breeding cycles which are not correlated with the time of year, and in these the individuals have intervals of less than a year between successive layings. Most of these species suffer from severe food shortages from time to time, and it seems as though they will breed at any time when there is sufficient food for the pair to get into breeding condition. They cannot predict what feeding conditions will be like for the young many weeks later. Here food acts as both the ultimate and the proximate factors controlling nesting. Even when food is obviously plentiful, as shown by large and regular feeds given to the young, some pairs will not be breeding. It seems that there must be a gap between the end of one breeding attempt and the start of the next. The most likely explanation is that birds must replace their feathers between breeding periods. Most seabirds do not breed and moult at the same time — presumably because any gaps in the wings and tail will impair their flight efficiency which must be at its highest when they have to collect food for themselves and their offspring. Also moulting birds have no ties to any one area and can move to wherever food is most plentiful. The boobies leave the colonies between breeding times and forage widely over the archipelago, Swallow-tailed Gulls and Waved Albatrosses migrate to the seas off Ecuador and Peru. It could be that the gonads need to recuperate between breeding attempts but this is unlikely as many birds only lay a single egg per nesting cycle, and the gonads would have several months to 'recover' even if there was continuous breeding.

Several species have annual breeding, and this is difficult to explain if there are no seasonal fluctuations in their food. The two with the shortest and most fixed laying periods, the Hawaiian Petrel and Waved Albatross, often feed far out to sea in areas where there may be such fluctuations in food. Masked Boobies and Great Frigatebirds have annual breeding but the cycles on different islands are out of phase, possibly due to the north and south movements of the Humboldt Current but more investigations are needed. It is interesting that the Masked Booby has also retained an annual nesting cycle on Ascension Island and Christmas Island (Central Pacific), where some other species have evolved more frequent breeding.

The two separate populations of Band-rumped Storm Petrels, each with

EGG LAYING DATES OF SEABIRDS

	MONTH												Intervals between successive layings
	J	F	M	A	M	J	J	A	S	O	N	D	
Galapagos Penguin	□	□	□	□	•	•	•	•	•	•	•	•	Often every 6 months
Waved Albatross			•	•	•	□	□						Annual
Audubon's Shearwater	•	•	•	•	•	•	•	•	•	•	•	•	About 9-10 months
Hawaiian Petrel		•	•	□	•	•	•						Annual
Band-rumped Storm Petrel	□	□		□								•	Annual
Wedge-rumped Storm Petrel		□	□			•	•						Annual
Red-billed Tropicbird (Plaza)	•	□				□		□	•	•	•	•	Annual
,, (Tower, Daphne)	•	•	•	•	•	•	•	•	•	•	•	•	Shorter than annual
Brown Pelican	•	•	•	•	•	•	•	•	•	•	•	•	Shorter than annual
Blue-footed Booby	•	•	•	•	□	•	•	•	•	•	•	•	Shorter than annual
Masked Booby	•	•	□	•	□	□	•	•	•	•	•	•	Annual
Red-footed Booby	•	•		•	•	•	•		•	•	•	•	Probably shorter than annual
Flightless Cormorant	□	□	•	•	•	•	•	•	•	□	□	□	Shorter than annual
Magnificent Frigatebird	□	□	□	□	•	•	•	•	•	•	•	□	Annual or longer
Great Frigatebird	•	•	•	•	•	•	•	•	•	•	•		Annual or longer
Lava Gull		□				•	□	□		□	□		Probably shorter than annual
Swallow-tailed Gull	•	•	•	•	•	•	•	•	•	•	•	•	About 9-10 months
Brown Noddy	•	•	•	•	•	•	•	•	•	□	•	•	Shorter than annual

• indicates many eggs,   □ few eggs. See notes under species for differences in breeding seasons between islands.

29

Breeding biology information on seabirds

	Incubation period (days)	Average incubation stint (days)	Fledging period (days)	Feeds per day to young	Fed after fledging (days)
Galapagos Penguin	40	2	60	1 +	0
Waved Albatross	60	5-22	167	0.4	0
Audubon's Shearwater	49	2-6	62	0.7	0
Hawaiian Petrel	52	10-13	110	0.5	0
Wedge-rumped Storm Petrel	?	5	76	0.5	0
Band-rumped Storm Petrel	42	6	73	0.7	0
Red-billed Tropicbird	42	6 +	85	1.0	0
Blue-footed Booby	41	0.7	105	1.8	56
Masked Booby	40	1.2	115	1.4	56
Red-footed Booby	45	5	130	0.9	91
Flightless Cormorant	35	0.2	60	3.6	120
Great Frigatebird	55	10	145	0.7	180 +
Magnificent Frigatebird	50	1-4	160	2.2	80 + +
Swallow-tailed Gull	33	0.5	65	1 +	25
Lava Gull	32	?	60	?	16

a fixed breeding régime, have probably evolved from a single breeding season by some out of season nesting which became successful, a situation which has been recorded in the Wedge-rumped Storm Petrel. But how the two seasons remain separate and have not given rise to continuous nesting, is a mystery.

The Red-billed Tropicbird has a rigid annual breeding cycle on Plaza, whereas a few miles away on Daphne there is breeding throughout the year with some birds having less than a year between layings. Perhaps at present these two breeding systems are about equally efficient at producing young.

WATERBIRDS

Apart from records of occupied nests, very little is known of the breeding of the birds restricted to the tide-edge, salt lagoons and freshwater, though it appears that most, if not all, can breed at any time of the year. It is difficult to see what factor might influence the breeding of the herons, but in the case of the Flamingo conditions in its salt-lagoon habitat are critical and must be just right before breeding is attempted. Both the White-cheeked Pintail and the Gallinule breed near semi-permanent ponds which are only full after heavy rains in the early part of some years. Elsewhere they can probably nest at any time.

LANDBIRDS

Scattered observations over many years, and systematic studies over three or four, have shown that Darwin's Finches in the arid parts of Galapagos normally breed sometime between December and March, the normal rainy season. If no rains materialise the finches do not breed, whereas in particularly wet years breeding will continue for most of the year. The effects of the first showers on the finches are spectacular. The males immediately start to sing, build display nests and try to attract females. Most flocks of birds disband and any birds which are in active moult arrest the moult and take up territories. If conditions continue to be good, breeding will commence and continue until there is a setback. Several broods may be raised and in wet years there is a vast increase in the numbers of finches, and previously rare species may become common. However, in a typical year, if there is such a thing in Galapagos, most pairs will raise but a single brood. Finches are capable of breeding at any time if conditions allow and birds with black bills, an indication of birds in breeding condition, are seen throughout the year. There are many resemblances between these finches and true desert birds, and in both cases rain is both the ultimate and proximate factors controlling nesting. Perhaps not surprisingly, the breeding seasons on different islands often do not coincide. The few observations on finches in the humid areas suggest a similarly-timed breeding season.

The rather unsatisfactory evidence for the other landbirds indicates that most species nest during the warm season, and, at least in the Yellow Warbler, they do so whether or not the rains materialise. In such species, rain is obviously not the proximate factor involved. Both the Galapagos Hawk and the Dove nest throughout the year but start many more nests just after the normal rains have finished. There would then be more birds and large insects for the Hawk. In the case of the Dove this is probably to take advantage of the large increase in seeds available after the growth of the many annual plants. During the rains this species may well be short of food as most intact seeds will have germinated and it is several weeks before any of the fresh crop of seeds become available.

Ecology

It is a well known ecological principle, known as Gause's Hypothesis, that animal species with exactly similar requirements cannot co-exist for any length of time. In most mainland areas with diverse faunas and floras, it is often difficult to show the differences between the closely related species which allow them to live side by side. The ecology of an oceanic island concerns few species, and in Galapagos it is often easy to see how the various bird species share out the resources.

Food is normally the critical factor. Not only can there be a difference in the actual food, but in how, when and where the food is obtained. All these factors help to reduce the competition between species. It must be pointed out that similar species can eat the same foods and behave identically in times of food abundance; it is only in times of shortage that it is imperative that there are differences.

SEABIRDS

The basic details of the feeding ecology of this group are given as a table; in most cases the differences between species are obvious. To a certain extent the size of the bird determines the size of its fish but there are still large overlaps. For instance, the boobies all eat similar prey caught by plunge-diving into the sea, often from a considerable height, but closer inspections of their habits have shown that they feed in difference areas. The Blue-footed Booby is adapted to foraging close inshore and can dive into very shallow water or even catch fish on the surface without actually entering the water; the Masked Booby tends to feed within the archipelago whereas the Red-footed Booby hunts well out to sea. Associated with the feeding ranges are differences in breeding biology. Blue-footed Boobies nest in at least 40 colonies, scattered throughout the islands; they are near to their food supplies and can, if conditions are good, catch sufficient food to raise two or even three young. The Red-footed Booby nests in five large colonies at the periphery of the islands as near as possible to the food but still the food is so far away that they can only ever hope to rear a single young, hence only a single egg is laid. The Masked Boody falls between the two, with about 25 fairly large colonies, and the birds lay a clutch of two eggs, though only a single young ever survives.

Bird	Food	How caught	Where
Galapagos Penguin	Small fish	Swimming under-water	Inshore, restricted range
Flightless Cormorant	Fish, eels, octopuses	Swimming under-water but fish taken from bottom	Inshore, restricted range
Waved Albatross	Large fish, squid	On the surface	Well offshore
Hawaiian Petrel	Fish and squid	On or near surface	Well offshore
Brown Pelican	Fish	Near surface by aerial diving	Inshore
Blue-footed Booby	Fish	Below surface by aerial diving	Inshore
Masked Booby	Fish	Below surface by aerial diving	Between and around islands
Red-footed Booby	Fish	Below surface by aerial diving	Well away from islands
Red-billed Tropicbird	Fish and squid	Below surface by aerial diving	Well away from islands
Swallow-tailed Gull	Fish and squid	Near surface at night	Between islands
Great Frigatebird	Fish	Either caught on surface or by chasing other seabirds	Well offshore
Magnificent Frigatebird	Fish	Either caught on surface or by chasing other seabirds	Between islands
Sooty Tern	Small fish	Picked from surface	Only feeds well away from land in warm seas
Brown Noddy	Small fish	Picked from surface — associates with predatory fish	Inshore
Audubon's Shearwater	Plankton, very small fish	On or just under the surface	Inshore
Band-rumped Storm Petrel	Plankton, very small fish	On surface when flying	Well away from islands — by day
Wedge-rumped Storm Petrel	Plankton, very small fish	On surface when flying	Between islands, by night
White-vented Storm Petrel	Plankton, very small fish	On surface when flying	Inshore by day
Lava Gull	Mainly a scavenger		

There are other methods of reducing competition. Red-tailed Tropic birds and Swallow-tailed Gulls eat identical food, but the former dives fo. its fish and squid far out to sea by day, and the latter feeds within the islands by night.

WATERBIRDS

There are obvious differences between the few species of water-birds Three species feed in salt lagoons. The Flamingo filters minute animals and algae from the water using its very specialised beak, the Stilt picks smal. animals from the mud with its long thin bill, and the White-cheeked Pintai. eats seeds. The Pintail and Gallinule are found together on a few freshwater ponds but the Gallinule eats more greenery and often dives for its food. Although not truly waterbirds, the rails might be considered here. As yet their food has not been studied but the Paint-billed Crake appears to prefer more open areas at slightly lower elevations than the endemic Galapagos Rail.

The herons are all common near the shore but only the Common Egret normally searches for its food on dry land. As might be expected the largest species, the Great Blue Heron, eats much larger prey than any of the others. We know little of the habits of the Striated Heron, but the Lava Heron catches fish by stealth or kingfisher-like diving. It also eats small crabs but does not compete with the crab-eating specialist, the Yellow-crowned Night Heron, as this hunts mainly by night and eats larger crabs. The rarity of the Oystercatcher is due to the paucity of suitable habitat, and not to competition as no other species feed on inter-tidal molluscs.

LANDBIRDS

There are three avian predators, the diurnal Hawk, the nocturnal Barn Owl and the more generalised Short-eared Owl which feeds by day on islands with no hawks and by night where hawks are present. Everywhere the Short-eared Owl eats more birds than does the Barn Owl.

The food preferences of the finches found on Santa Cruz are well known due to the studies of Bowman. These, and more general observations on finches which do not occur on this island, are given in the table. Differences between the Warbler Finch and the Yellow Warbler have yet to be demonstrated but the Yellow Warbler is rarely seen in areas without greenery and the Warbler Finch is sometimes common in such areas.

LANDBIRDS

Mockingbird	Omnivorous
Dark-billed Cuckoo	Insects, large caterpillars
Galapagos Martin	Insects caught in flight, often high in air
Vermilion Flycatcher	Insects caught in flight near ground. Prefers green areas
Large-billed Flycatcher	Insects caught in flight near ground. Often in dry areas
Yellow Warbler	Insects picked from leaves ⎤ Separation unknown
Warbler Finch	Insects picked from leaves ⎦
Mangrove Finch	Large insects in mangrove areas
Woodpecker Finch	Largish insects, usually hidden. Uses tool
Large Tree Finch	Largish insects — rather similar to above but from softer wood
Medium Tree Finch	Imperfectly known — many insects and fruits. Occurs only on Floreana
Small Tree Finch	Small insects, fruits and seeds. Can exist in drier areas than other tree finches
Vegetarian Finch	Entirely vegetarian
Large Ground Finch	Very hard seeds
Medium Ground Finch	Moderately hard seeds
Small Ground Finch	Moderately soft seeds ⎤ Sometimes occur on same island but not in same vegetation zone
Sharp-beaked Ground Finch	Moderately soft seeds ⎦
Cactus Finch	Seeds — usually associated with Prickly Pear cacti ⎤ Never occur on same island
Large Cactus Finch	Seeds — including very hard ⎦
Galapagos Dove	Small seeds

Changes in the avifauna and its conservation

As far as is known no indigenous Galapagos bird species has become extinct, but some species are no longer found on individual islands where they previously occurred.

Even today after much intensive fieldwork, it is often difficult to be certain of the distribution of some landbirds. The large fluctuations in their numbers mean that a rare species may be overlooked for several years. There are even greater difficulties in evaluating the older records. Unfortunately the oldest records, when man was just starting to clear land, are those of Darwin, who at first did not realise the significance of accurately labelling which islands his specimens came from. However some species collected by him do not now exist on the islands which he visited.

During the years 1835-1929, 14 species were collected on major islands where they are now missing. The best example concerns the 1905-6 Academy expedition. They spent but a few hours on Wenman and visited just a small area near the base of the cliffs, yet they brought back a total of 13 individuals of five species (Medium and Small Ground Finches, Small Tree Finch, Large-billed and Vermilion Flycatchers) which have not been found there since. This expedition also took unique records on Hood (Medium Ground Finch), Tower (Large-billed Flycatcher) and Barrington (Dark-billed Cuckoo), and saw or collected 12 landbirds way out at sea. It is impossible to know whether these old island records refer to stragglers from other islands or to now extinct populations, but they suggest that some things have changed. Unfortunately there are no reliable weather records from the start of this century, but the older settlers on Santa Cruz agree that conditions then were far wetter than at present.

The most recent loss, during the 1930s, was the Sharp-beaked Ground Finch from Santa Cruz. The species inhabited the humid highlands, parts of which were cleared for agriculture at this time but only a very small proportion of the available habitat was removed. The Sharp-beaked Finch is also now missing from San Cristóbal, Floreana and Isabela; all islands which would appear to be suitable and where specimens were collected in 1897, 1835, 1880, and 1901 respectively. Perhaps man, in his cultivation of areas of these islands, brought about some slight change in the environment resulting in these extinctions. Similarly puzzling is the disappearance of the mockingbird from the main island of Floreana. It has

)een suggested that introduced cats were responsible but this seems unlikely as mockingbirds on other islands have adjusted to introduced animals.

Man exterminated the endemic Hawk on San Cristóbal and probably Floreana and reduce the species to the verge of extinction on Santa Cruz. Introduced goats removed much of the greenery from Barrington and this, along with a slight change in climate may have resulted in the island losing Vermilion Flycatcher and Large Tree Finch. Similarly goats changed Pinta from a very densely vegetated island to open parkland, resulting in a dramatic decline in the population of Galapagos Rails. The vegetation on Pinta has now recovered following the killing of many goats and the rail is common again.

The Hawaiian Petrel is endemic to Hawaii, where it is rare, and to the moist highlands of several islands in the Galapagos. In both archipelagos it is endangered by land clearance, introduced mammals, or both. Although still fairly common in Galapagos, the future seems uncertain for some nesting areas, thickly vegetated parts of the highlands with good soil have been taken for agriculture, the eggs and young are killed by black rats, and the adults destroyed by pigs and dogs. Nesting success is so low, and the adult mortality so high, that there must be great concern for the species.

The only recent coloniser of the islands is the Paint-billed Crake, which was first discovered in 1953 and is now known to breed on several islands. Possibly the opening up of land by cattle and agriculture have produced a previously lacking suitable habitat.

CONSERVATION

The changes in the birds of the islands given above make gloomy reading, but, apart from the Hawaiian Petrel, we can hope with reasonably certainty for a better future. There is, however, no room for complacency for several of the populations are very small—

Galapagos Penguin	a few thousand individuals
Flightless Cormorant	800 pairs
Galapagos Hawk	130 pairs
Flamingo	500-1,000 birds
Lava Gull	less than 400 pairs

and most have restricted ranges. It seems possible that the Hawk might be able to recolonise some areas from which it has been removed and there is no reason to suppose that the other species were ever any commoner than they now are. Still the thoughtless use of nets set for crayfish in the waters around Fernandina could easily decimate the populations of Flightless Cormorants and Galapagos Penguins. Harassment of the Flamingos by over-zealous bird watchers and photographers also could have serious consequences.

It is easy to be depressed about the future. The increase in human population, the spread of agriculture, the defoliation of islands by goats, the destruction of animals by introduced rats, pigs, dogs and cats, are obvious threats. Nevertheless, it is not too late to save most of the islands.

In the 1950s the scientific world awoke to the realization that, unless urgent action was taken, Galapagos would cease to be the world's outstanding "natural laboratory" for the study of organic evolution. So in 1959 an international body, the Charles Darwin Foundation, was set up under the sponsorship of UNESCO and IUCN with the financial support of individuals from many countries. The foundation offers facilities for scientists to work at its research station at Academy Bay and advises the Government of Ecuador on conservation matters. The Government has set aside nine tenths of the archipelago as a National Park and nature reserve and created a vigorous National Park Service to implement its protective measures. As a result of the close collaboration between the two bodies, the tide of degradation of the islands has not only been halted but actually turned back in many areas.

Endangered races of giant tortoises and land iguanas have been rescued by breeding them in captivity at the station. Goats have been reduced or eliminated on several islands, where the vegetation is now regenerating. The local population receives education in the aims of conservation. Scientists permanently monitor the impact of the growing numbers of tourists, to watch whether they are harming the birds, mammals, reptiles or plants. Much valuable research has been carried out by hundreds of scientific missions from every continent. There is still so much that needs to be done to protect these fabulous islands but, given generous public support, the Galapagos can be made safe for posterity.

Galapagos animals are strikingly tame and tolerant of man. Whether they are to remain so depends on the conduct of visitors to the islands.

Please treat the islands with the respect which they deserve.

Migrants

More species have been recorded as migrants or vagrants than breed within the islands, and during the northern winter migrant birds form a very important part of the Galapagos avifauna. However, the distribution of migrants is very uneven, the vast majority being restricted to the coastal areas.

Thirty species of migrant wader have been recorded, contrasting with the two breeding species (Oystercatcher and Common Stilt which are also in different families to the migrants). This is to be expected as many wader species breed in North America and winter along the western shore of South America and are used to undertaking long sea crossings as a normal part of their migration. About twenty of these species may be considered as regular visitors, though the numbers of any one species may vary greatly from year to year, but Galapagos is an important wintering ground for only six species — Semipalmated Plover, Ruddy Turnstone, Wandering Tattler, Sanderling, Whimbrel and Northern Phalarope. Small numbers of the commoner species remain in the islands during the northern summer and may attain breeding plumage.

In most years there are a few records of hirundines and Bobolinks, but other landbirds are very rare, there being a total of 20 records divided between seven species. Cocos Island, which lies 425 miles to the N.E. and has received far less attention from ornithologists, boasts a list of no less than two species of flycatchers, 12 parulid warblers, two icterids, one sparrow, and two nighthanks. Cocos Island is probably on the edge of the distributional range, and at the limits of endurance of many passerines, so that birds reaching Cocos Island may be unwilling or unable to continue any farther, and any completely lost birds will not be able to survive the journey of at least 800 miles from Central America to Galapagos. This of course assumes that birds do not make the shortest crossing—the 600 miles from Ecuador to the Galapagos.

Several seabirds occur as regular migrants, the commonest being Franklin's Gull, Royal and Common/Arctic Terns, but surprisingly the only oceanic species to occur with any regularity are Sooty Shearwater and Cape Pigeon. However, Leach's Storm Petrel may be much commoner than the few records suggest. The other storm petrels, the jaegers, Skua, and the shearwaters are probably best classified as vagrants though some are common just outside our area. In exceptional years some of these species may be seen within the islands. In 1972 Cape Pigeons, Sooty Shearwaters, Flesh-footed Shearwaters, Common/Arctic Terns and Red Phalaropes were all seen in unprecedented numbers, presumably due to some change in oceangraphical conditions associated with 'El Niño'.

Almost all migrants to Galapagos have their origin in North or Central America, but a few species could arrive from South America, e.g. Groove-billed Ani, Black-bellied Tree Duck and Cattle Egret. The accidentals include birds from as far away as southern South America (Southern Skua), and New Zealand (Black Petrel). In a few cases it is impossible to know the area of origin; the Peregrines are probably of North American stock but a few could come from the extreme South American populations which migrate north at least as far as Ecuador.

Many of the migrants enter habitats where there are few if any native birds. For instance Wandering Tattlers occur in large numbers on the rocky shores where there are no resident species. This must indicate a sufficiency of food so why are there no native birds to utilise these resources? The few Peregrines which reach the islands are in a bird-eating hawk's paradise, so why is there not a resident falcon? Some species occur with such frequency that they should be able to colonise the area. Only time and many more studies will tell what limits the range of some of these birds.

In conclusion it appears that relatively few species can be classified as true migrants, most are at the best accidentals, and some are obviously completey lost vagrants with no hope of ever returning to their home area.

The birds likely to be seen

Probably the most enjoyment in bird-watching comes from finding and identifying birds for one's self. However, for most people, their trip will be an all too brief, once in a lifetime experience. It takes practice to be able to identify even the majority of the finches, but it does help to know what is to be expected at any one place.

The notes below include the majority of species likely to be seen at the most visited places. Odd migrants may occur anywhere but it is extremely rare for any of the resident landbirds to be seen outside their normal range.

SANTA CRUZ

A visit to Academy Bay, on the southern coast, and a walk for a few hours inland, gives a good cross-section of both Galapagos landbirds and vegetation.

All the normal shorebirds can be seen on the tidal margin, and Noddies and an odd pair of Galapagos Martins nest on the cliffs near to the village. In the village birds often became very tame; Yellow Warblers and Great Blue Herons will enter houses in search of food. Common Egrets and Night Herons walk between the houses and Stilts feed in the small village lagoon. The mangroves near the jetty are the only place where the Belted Kingfisher is reported with any regularity.

Finches are the most obvious birds in the arid zone, with Cactus, Small and Medium Ground Finches all being abundant. Great care must be taken with identification of the Large Ground Finch on this island as some of the larger-billed individuals of the Medium Ground Finch are virtually indistinguishable; if seen in a flock, large beaked Ground Finches can safely be assumed to be the Medium species. Vegetarian and the Small Tree Finches are not uncommon though rather more typical of moister areas. In wet seasons a few Warbler Finches might also be encountered. Near the coast the Large-billed Flycatcher is commoner than the Vermilion though even this is not too common.

If at all possible an excursion inland to Bellavista should be taken. At first the trail rises slowly, but by the time the last Prickly Pear Cacti have been passed, the Small Tree, Vegetarian and Warbler Finches have become commoner and the Cactus Finch rather rare. Higher up both of the

41

Flycatchers and the Dark-billed Cuckoo should be encountered and the chances of seeing a Woodpecker Finch increase greatly. If more time is available go by road to Bellavista and walk up to Media Luna at the upper edge of the Miconia zone. Here is a likely place to see Woodpecker and Large Tree Finches, and the Galapagos Rail will be heard calling from the thick undergrowth. Slightly lower the Paint-billed Crake also occurs but high up it is far less common than the endemic species. This high area is the nesting place of the Hawaiian Petrels.

Farther to the west lies the tortoise reserve. During and after the heavy rains there are freshwater ponds which attract Gallinules and ducks. Both species of rail occur, with the Paint-billed being the commoner. At night Barn and Short-eared Owls may be seen.

SOUTH PLAZA

This island, which lies about half a mile off the eastern tip of Santa Cruz, receives more visitors than any other island in the Galapagos. But this does not detract from its charm or attraction. It is small, only a half mile long by 150 yards wide, and flat except for the southern edge which is bounded by cliffs up to 50 feet high where all but a handful of the seabirds nest. The western third of the island is covered by thorn scrub and cacti, the nesting habitat of Cactus, Small and Medium Ground Finches and Yellow Warblers. The mockingbird has not been recorded and the Large-billed Flycatcher has been only once noted breeding.

Five species of seabirds regularly nest and all have been studied in detail for many years. Indeed probably more is known of the seabirds of Plaza than of any other tropical island. Five species breed; Swallow-tailed Gull (ca. 400 pairs nesting among the cliff boulders and ledges), Audubon's Shearwaters (500 pairs in holes in the cliffs), Band-rumped Storm Petrels (1,000 pairs in the cliffs; nocturnal, so rarely seen), Red-billed Tropicbirds (50 pairs in the cliffs) and a handful of Noddies (on exposed cliffs). Brown Pelicans have bred on North Plaza and a single pair of Masked Boobies nested once on South Plaza, but these two species, along with Blue-footed Boobies and Frigatebirds, are always to be seen on the island. White-vented and, less commonly, Wedge-rumped Storm Petrels are often seen close inshore and during the winter they are joined by flocks of Northern Phalaropes.

Shorebirds include Yellow-crowned Night Heron and Lava Heron (both of which breed), Great Blue Heron, occasional Egrets and Lava Gulls. A small flock of Whimbrel, Turnstone, Wandering Tattler, Sanderling is present throughout the year, and this is sometimes joined by Black-bellied and Semipalmated Plovers and Oystercatchers. One or two Short-eared Owls visit the island nightly to feed on the Storm Petrels and Shearwaters.

Neighbouring North Plaza has the same bird species but is difficult to move around on due to the thick vegetation.

TOWER

Visitors are enticed to Darwin Bay by the very large numbers of Red-footed Boobies and Frigatebirds, but there are good numbers of other species. The vast majority of the frigates are Great Frigatebirds but some Magnificent Frigatebirds also nest inland near the crater. Although odd frigates can be seen displaying from January to July, the peak of activity occurs March to June. Red-footed Boobies are always present but their breeding is very erratic and in some years there is no nesting at all. In contrast the Masked Boobies have eggs between August and December. The deep waters around the island are not suitable for Blue-footed Boobies, although they have nested at least twice, or Pelicans, but one or two individuals of these species are often seen in the bay.

Swallow-tailed Gulls, Audubon's Shearwaters, and Red-billed Tropic-birds nest in the cliffs and very large numbers of Wedge-rumped Storm Petrels can be seen flying by day above their colony on the south-eastern coast of the island. Band-rumped Storm Petrels also nest but their presence is only indicated by the prey remains of the relatively common and diurnal Short-eared Owl. The sea lagoon at the landing beach is a favourite haunt of Yellow-crowned Night Herons, Wandering Tattlers, Turnstones, Whimbrels and a flock of Lava Gulls. Occasional White-cheeked Pintail also occur here and at the crater lake.

Although there are only four species of finch on Tower they are of great interest and this is the easiest place to see the Large Ground Finch (located by loud and rather slow song) and the Sharp-beaked Ground Finch. The two other species are the smaller billed of the two subspecies of Large Cactus Finch and the Warbler Finch. Normally these species must be looked for in the bush but they well repay a short walk inland. Yellow Warblers, Galapagos Mockingbirds and the Dove also occur but there is no flycatcher.

JAMES

Although there are a few little-known areas on the northern coast, James Bay at the north-western corner is probably of the most ornithological interest. Two places are normally visited — the salt lagoon at Espumilla and the furseal colony near the now-defunct salt-mine.

Waterbirds are well represented in both areas. Espumilla normally has a few Flamingos, White-cheeked Pintails, Common Stilts, Semipalmated Plovers and, during the northern winter, Northern and Wilson's Phalaropes. The shore near the furseals should produce herons, Oyster-catchers, and a good selection of waders, such as Wandering Tattler, Black-bellied and Semipalmated Plovers, Whimbrel, Sanderling, Turnstone and sometimes a rarity. Flamingos, Stilts and the Pintail occur on the lake inland in the salt-mine crater. Small and Medium Ground Finches, Cactus Finches, Galapagos Mockingbirds and Doves, are common and it is usually possible to see both the Vermilion and Large-billed Flycatchers, and the Hawk by a short walk inland. This is one of the few places on James where the cuckoo is seen. Galapagos Martins sweep in front of the cliffs near the salt-mine landing and at nearby Buccaneer Bay.

HOOD

Most visitors land at Punta Suarez, at the extreme western tip of the island. Although the main attractions are the seabirds, the first birds to be seen will be the endemic Hood Mockingbird and the Galapagos Dove. It is well worthwhile paying attention to the finches, for although there are only three species they are very interesting. Only on Hood can the large-billed race of the Large Cactus Finch be seen, and the Warbler Finch (a very grey subspecies) is far commoner than the much brighter Yellow Warbler. The other nesting passerines are the Small Ground Finch and the Large-billed Flycatcher (commoner inland in scrubby areas).

The colony of Blue-footed Boobies extends over a large area and there are always some birds nesting. In contrast the Masked Boobies, which have their colonies right on the cliff-edge, have an annual breeding cycle with the eggs laid from November, and the last young fledging in June.

Probably the main attraction of Hood is the Waved Albatross. Although it is only necessary to walk for a third of a mile to reach the first nesting group of some 300 pairs, the colony at Punta Suarez extends along the coast for several miles and has several thousand pairs. The first birds return to the colonies in late March and the last young leave in early January, so there are several months when the colonies are deserted. Part of the attraction of these birds is their complicated display so it should be stressed that the display is mainly concerned with courting and pair formation, rather than mating, so that display is far commoner late in the breeding cycle when birds are either finding mates for the next season or reinforcing their pair-bonds, rather than during the laying period.

Other seabirds to be seen are the Swallow-tailed Gull, Red-billed Tropicbird, a few Audubon's Shearwaters (all of which nest in the cliffs) and both species of Frigatebirds (which, however, do not breed at Suarez). Remains of the nocturnal Band-rumped Storm Petrel may also be seen — prey of the Short-eared Owl. A pair of Hawks nest inland but hunt for doves, lizards, iguanas, and mockingbirds near the point.

Hood has more Oystercatchers than any other island and two pairs breed on Punta Suarez. Please take care not to disturb these birds as their eggs are easy prey for the Mockingbirds. Other shorebirds likely to be seen are Yellow-crowned Night Heron, Lava Heron, and migrant Turnstone, Wandering Tattler and Whimbrel.

The other tip of Hood, Punta Cevallos, has large seabird colonies, but the landings can be very difficult. The Great Frigatebird nests in this area. Gardner Bay is of little interest except for landbirds. Considering the few observers and visits, Hood has supplied an unexpected number of rare migrants including Summer Tanager and the only Black-billed Cuckoo and Chimney Swift and four Common Nighthawks. Migrant hirundines are more often recorded at Punta Suarez than at any other place.

FERNANDINA

Due to the rugged and barren lava, there are only a few places on Fernandina where more than a few species of coastal birds can be expected. Probably the most attractive areas are the mangroves, lagoons and sandy point on the north-east corner, Punta Espinosa. Here there are several of the typically small colonies of Flightless Cormorants and Galapagos Penguins; birds may be found nesting at any time of year. The mangroves are the nesting places for many Pelicans, a few pairs of Great Blue Herons, some Galapagos Mockingbirds and Yellow Warblers. Both the Galapagos Rail and Mangrove Finch have been reported but not for several years. The only finch seen with any regularity is the Small Ground Finch. Doves are common and sometimes there is a pair of Vermilion Flycatchers. The local pair of Hawks spend much time surveying their territory from the dead mangroves on the Point. Other species of landbirds are common on Fernandina but they are almost entirely restricted to the vegetation high up on the volcano's rim — far out of reach of all but the most intrepid.

Shorebirds include Yellow-crowned Night Heron, Lava and Striated Herons (note intermediates), Oystercatchers and migrant waders. Seabirds seen close inshore include White-vented and Wedge-rumped Storm Petrels, Northern Phalaropes, and Blue-footed Boobies. At night Frigatebirds sleep in the mangroves and flocks of Audubon's Shearwaters fly inland to roost under the barren lava.

The Mangrove Finch is the most elusive bird in the Galapagos; although it has recently been seen at Punta Mangle, the best chance to see it is to visit the large mangrove areas between Caleta Black and Punta Tortuga (western Isabela directly opposite Punta Espinosa). Even then one needs a good measure of luck. Slightly farther south, Tagus Cove is a good place to see Galapagos Martins, Penguins and Flightless Cormorants from the sea.

FLOREANA

Ornithologically this is an interesting island and it is unfortunate that most visitors confine their activities to the coast. The lagoon at Punta Cormorant has Flamingos, White-cheeked Pintail, Common Stilts and other waders. Turnstone, Whimbrel, Wandering Tattler, Semipalmated Plover and Sanderling occur throughout the year, and are joined September to April by Northern and Wilson's Phalaropes, Black-bellied Plover and Least Sandpiper, and not infrequently by less common species such as Lesser Yellowlegs and small sandpipers.

The islands off the northern and eastern shores have a good selection of seabirds. Gardner-near-Floreana is the only place in the archipelago where the three species of boobies and both frigates normally nest side-by-side. The Charles Mockingbird is now only found on Gardner and Champion. Small and Medium Ground Finches and Cactus Finches are abundant in the coastal areas and the Large-billed Flycatcher and Dark-billed Cuckoo can normally be found.

A visit to the highlands entails a two hour walk inland from Black Beach but the trail is good. Once the Guava and Scalesia areas are reached tree finches replace the ground finches as the commonest birds. Floreana is the only island with the Medium Tree Finch (which is very common), and also has the Large (rather uncommon) and the Small species. The Vegetarian Finch, Yellow Warbler, Dark-billed Cuckoo and both flycatchers are abundant. The Warbler Finch varies greatly in numbers — some years it is common, others virtually missing. The ponds hold ducks and Gallinules and the Galapagos Rail and Paint-billed Crake breed.

VILLAMIL

This settlement on the southern coast of Isabela, is seldom visited by tourists as it has little of any general interest and the landing is sometimes difficult. However, as far as waterbirds are concerned it is far and away the best area in the archipelago. Salt and brackish lagoons, rocky and muddy shores, and long sandy beaches all close together are very attractive to migrant waders, more than 20 species of which have been identified here.

The lagoon on the edge of the village can usually produce tame Flamingos, and is one of the few areas where Gallinules occur in any numbers. There will also be White-cheeked Pintails, Black-bellied and Semipalmated Plovers, Least Sandpipers, Common Stilts. A walk for a mile or so along the beach will produce a good selection of waders and close offshore will normally be seen Royal and Common/Arctic Terns. Franklin's Gulls feed among the large concentration of Lava Gulls.

GUAYAQUIL TO GALAPAGOS

Many of the species described later will be seen — especially Waved Albatross, Cape Pigeon, Sooty Shearwater, Hawaiian and White-chinned Petrels, Wedge-rumped and Black Storm Petrels, Red-billed Tropicbird, boobies, frigatebirds, Swallow-tailed Gull, terns, Pomarine Jaeger and Northern Phalarope. In addition Sabine's Gull *Xema sabini* (smaller than Swallow-tailed, solid black wedges an outer wings, forked tail) and Hornby's Storm Petrel *Oceanodroma hornbyi* (upperparts grey-brown with white collar, underparts white with dark breast band) are regularly recorded. In the exceptional 'El Niño' years many other species appear, including Black-browed Albatross *Diomedea melanophris* (solid black wings), Southern Fulmar *Fulmarus glacialoides* (pearl grey) and Peruvian Booby *Sula variegata* (white with mottled lower back and tail, wings brownish black).

The Birds

SPHENISCIDAE: Penguins

GALAPAGOS PENGUIN *Spheniscus mendiculus*

Local name Pingüino

Identification: 1.19", height 14".Unmistakable: the only penguin in the area. Adults have back, head and flippers blue-black in fresh plumage, brown when worn. Underparts white except for a black line along the sides and scattered feathers on the breast. Immatures greyer, with pale grey patch on side of head and chin. Bill dark with a pinkish, unfeathered area at the base.

Voice: A donkey-like braying.

Food: Small fish, caught by swimming under water.

Breeding: Colonial, though individual colonies are often small and the pairs widely separated. Two whitish eggs laid in a hole under lava. Nesting occurs at all times of year with some pairs breeding every six months if

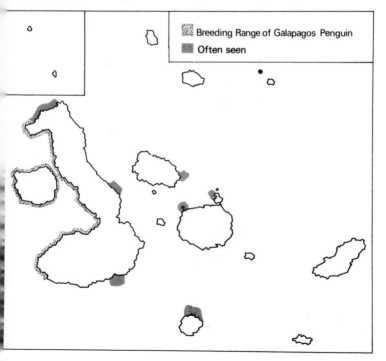

Breeding Range of Galapagos Penguin

Often seen

conditions are suitable. Much of the activity at a colony occurs at night.

Distribution: Breeds in suitable areas around the coasts of Fernandina and Isabela (on the west side from just north of Cape Berkeley to Iguana Cove). Birds, usually immatures, sometimes seen eastern Isabela, James, Bartolomé (where display and mating seen), north Santa Cruz and Floreana; rare elsewhere. Total population a few thousand birds, Endemic

Adult Galapagos Penguins

Waved Albatross display

52

PODICIPEDIDAE: Grebes

PIED-BILLED GREBE *Podilymbus podiceps* **pl. 3**

Identification: 1. 14″. General appearance like a stocky, tailless duck. Upperparts brown-grey, underparts whitish, undertail coverts white. Bill rather chicken-like and horn coloured or white with vertical black band. Rarely seen to fly, prefers to escape by diving.

Distribution: Three records in mangrove lagoons at Academy Bay (Santa Cruz), one at Pta. Moreno (Isabela). The species is widespread in the Americas. Northern breeding birds migrate south, southern breeders migrate north.

DIOMEDEIDAE: Albatrosses

WAVED ALBATROSS *Diomedea irrorata* **pl. 1**

Local name Albatros

Identification: 1. 34″, w.s. 7-8′. By far the largest Galapagos bird, weighing 7-11 lb. Upperparts, including wings and end of tail, brown, contrasting with white head, neck and underparts. Pale rump barred with brown. In flight appears a brown bird with white foreparts, large yellow bill, and short tail. Adult has golden tinge to head and neck. Juvenile as adult but bill pale horn colour.

Flight: Like all albatrosses a good glider given sufficient wind but, due to the relatively calm conditions in Galapagos, flaps more than other species.

Voice: In display a loud, prolonged 'whoo-oo'.

Food: Fish, squid and a few other invertebrates. Sometimes joins frigatebirds in attacking boobies.

Breeding: Colonial. A single white egg laid mid-April to June, the last young fledge in January. In some years breeding may fail completely and large numbers of abandoned eggs litter the colonies. Sometimes first breeds at three years, most not until five or six, adult survival is 96% per year, giving average life span of about 30 years.

Displays between adults are commonest late in the nesting period and are associated with pair formation for breeding the following year and not with mating.

Distribution: Breeds on Hood with colonies at Punta Suarez, Punta Cevallos, and along the southern coast and inland on the south facing slopes of the highest hills. Total population about 12,000 pairs. The birds are not present from mid-January until mid-March when they are at sea off Ecuador and Peru. A few pairs also breed on Isla de la Plata, off Ecuador.

WANDERING/ROYAL ALBATROSS
Diomedea exulans/epomophora

Identification: 1. 45", w.s. 10-11'. These 'Great' Albatrosses are among the largest flying birds. Plumage varies with age but generally black and white, with the white back contrasting with mainly dark upper wings Specific identification difficult but immature Wandering Albatrosses have many dark feathers in wings and tail. Wandering Albatrosses follow ships, Royal Albatrosses do not.

Flight: Majestic, rarely flaps; bird appears hunch-backed.

Distribution: Two records. Breed subantarctic islands and New Zealand, disperse widely into temperate regions.

BLACK-FOOTED ALBATROSS *Diomedea nigripes*

Identification: 1. 28", w.s. 6.5'. Mainly sooty-brown with white area around base of bill, immature also has whitish upper tail coverts. Follows ships.

Distribution: One record, also between Galapagos and mainland. A black albatross seen on Hood in 1897 could have been this species. Nests on Hawaiian islands, disperses widely over North Pacific.

PROCELLARIIDAE: Typical petrels and shearwaters

GIANT PETREL *Macronectes sp.*
Identification: 1. 34″, w.s. 7′. Plumage variable, adult usually grey-brown, paler on head; immature all-dark. Bill very large, tip green in *M. giganteus,* pink or yellow-brown in *M. halli.* These species are extremely difficult to separate.
Flight: Like an ungainly albatross. Regularly follows ships.
Distribution: Once. Breed in Antarctica and sub-antarctica, disperse widely at sea. *M. giganteus* migrates north in Humboldt Current.

CAPE PIGEON *Daption capense*
Identification: 1. 15″, w.s. 35″. Easily identified, black and white patched seabird. Head and neck black or very dark sooty grey, remainder of upperparts chequered black and white. Underparts white with throat either white or black. Two white patches on each wing and black tail band. Underwings white, edged with black.
Flight: Strong, periods of flapping alternating with glides near the surface of the sea. Often follows ships.
Distribution: Some years regularly seen in small numbers; also between Galapagos and the mainland. The species breeds on islands near Antarctica and migrates north.

Cape Pigeon

HAWAIIAN (DARK-RUMPED) PETREL   pl. 1

Pterodroma phaeopygia

Local name Pata pegada

Identification: 1. 17″, w.s. 36″. Much larger than commoner Audubon's Shearwater. Black upperparts contrast with white underparts, white sides to the rump and conspiciously white forehead. Underwings white, edged with black. Bill heavy, hooked and black.

Flight: Diagnostic. In calm conditions, birds gain a little height by flapping and then glide a considerable distance. In windy conditions birds rarely flap but glide in long arcs, often curving high above the water. The wings are held slightly crooked.

Voice: Often heard calling at night 'kee-kee-kee — (c)ooo'.

Food: Fish and squid usually caught well away from the islands.

Breeding: Colonial. Single white egg laid in a deep earthy barrow, on Santa Cruz June to August but on Floreana February to March.

Distribution: Nests in the humid and thickly vegetated uplands of Santa Cruz, James, San Cristóbal, Floreana and Isabela (Santo Tomas, Alcedo). Not uncommon at sea (except December to March) but rarely seen on land as is nocturnal at the breeding areas. Often heard calling at night and birds seen at dusk and dawn flying between the sea and the highlands. The species is declining in Galapagos due to the depredations of feral dogs, pigs and rats, and destruction of the nesting areas. On Hawaii, another subspecies is in danger of extinction.

BLACK PETREL *Procellaria parkinsoni*

Identification: 1. 18″. An entirely sooty black shearwater except shafts of primaries show white below. Bill horn or greenish with black tip; legs and feet black.

Distribution: Three specimens collected 1905-6 are the only records for this part of the Pacific. Breeds on islands off New Zealand.

WEDGE-TAILED SHEARWATER *Puffinus pacificus*

Identification: 1. 17″, w.s. 38″. A large shearwater with upper surface dark brown, under surface including underwings either white (in the pale phase) or dark (dark phase). Tail long and obviously wedge-shaped. Bill grey or pink.

Flight: Graceful with long glides interspaced with few shallow wing beats, wings kept slightly bent.

Distribution: The only definite record is of a bird found eaten by a Short-eared Owl on Plaza, but the species is not uncommon to the north and north-east of the archipelago. Nests on most island groups in the tropical Pacific.

Remarks: Great care must be taken with the identification of larger shearwaters as several other species could occur.

Wedge-tailed Shearwater

FLESH-FOOTED SHEARWATER *Puffinus carneipes*
Identification: 1. 19″, w.s. to 43″. Large, heavily built shearwater; upperparts greyish brown, underparts variable, white to grey, palest on belly and breast (or all dark in Australian and New Zealand race). Heavy bill diagnostically straw coloured with dark tip. Legs and feet pale. Told from Wedge-tailed by shorter tail, heavier build and pale beak, and dark phase from Sooty by beak colour and broader wings.
Flight: Rather laboured, alternating periods of flapping and gliding. Wings held straight.
Distribution: Two records in 1972 refer to the race (or perhaps a distinct species Pink-footed Shearwater *P. creatopus*) which breeds on Juan Fernandez and other Chilean islands and migrates north. Another race (sometimes referred to a separate species, Pale-footed Shearwater) nests in Australia and New Zealand and could occur in the area.

SOOTY SHEARWATER *Puffinus griseus*
Identification: 1. 19″, w.s. to 43″. At a distance appears all black but is blackish brown with underparts slightly paler. Good field mark is the greyish-white underwing. Rather slender bill black, legs and feet usually dark. Tail rather short not pointed.

Sooty Shearwater

Flight: More laboured than some of the other shearwaters, with more flapping, and closer to the water. Wings held straight and not crooked.

Distribution: A regular visitor in small numbers, common between Galapagos and Ecuador. Breeds on islands around southern South America, Australia and New Zealand, migrates north.

Note: White-chinned Petrel *Procellaria aequinoctialis,* slightly stockier and larger (21″) but also all-black except for inconspicuous white chin, and pale beak, occurs off Ecuador. Follows ships.

AUDUBON'S SHEARWATER *Puffinus lherminieri* pl. 1

Identification: 1. 12″, w.s. 27″. Very common, medium-sized seabird with blackish upperparts and pure white underneath. Black top of head and white chin and throat give the bird a capped appearance. Bill long and thin, hooked tip.

Flight: Close to the sea, periods of flapping alternating with frequent glides. The normal flight is level and direct (the Hawaiian Petrel twists and banks).

Voice: A loud 'kee-kaa-cooo' usually given when birds sweeping in front of the nesting cliffs, less commonly when feeding or going to roost.

Food: Small planktonic crustacea and fish larvae. Often feed in large flocks in association with Noddy Terns and Pelicans.

Breeding: Colonial. A single white egg laid in a hole in a seacliff. Breeding occurs in all months and individual pairs can nest every nine or ten months if successful in raising a young, otherwise more frequently. Adult survival 93% between breeding cycles. Noisy communal displays precede breeding. Diurnal at the breeding colonies. Often preyed upon by the Short-eared Owl.

Distribution: Common breeder on the smaller islets and the cliffs of the larger islands. Large nocturnal roosts inland in the lava fields of Fernandina. Although seen throughout the archipelago it is commonest in coastal waters. Widespread in tropical oceans.

Audubon's Shearwater

DOVE PRION *Pachyptila desolata*
Identification: 1. 10″. A prion is a small blue-grey seabird with a dark W across the wings and black band on end of tail. Specific identifications of the several species are extremely difficult as they are based on bill characters.
Flight: Erratic.
Distribution: Single dead on Floreana. Prions breed on southern islands — and some migrate northwards.

HYDROBATIDAE: Storm petrels

WHITE-VENTED (ELLIOT'S) STORM PETREL   pl. 1
Oceanites gracilis
Local name for storm petrel Golondrina de mar or de tormenta.
Identification: 1. 6″, w.s. 10″. Appears smaller than the other storm petrels, with more rounded wings, square-ended tail and long legs. In flight feet project behind tail. Plumage all-black except for white rump patch and white or grey stripe along the centre of underparts from lower breast to vent. All storm petrels have very pronounced tubular nostrils.
Flight: Usually identifiable by the rapid wing beats and the direct, level flight. It is this species which normally feeds by 'walking-on-the-water'.
Food: Planktonic animals and scraps of fish killed by sealions, whales and man.
Breeding: Has never been found breeding but the Galapagos subspecies is endemic and resident. Examination of dead birds suggests that the species lays during the cold season (April-September).
Distribution: The commonest storm petrel inshore in Galapagos. Endemic to the Humboldt Current; another race is found off Peru and Chile.

WHITE-FACED STORM PETREL *Pelagodroma marina*   pl. 1
Identification: 1. 8″. Very different to the other recorded storm petrels. Upperparts dark grey, slightly darker on the wings. All undersurface white though occasionally some dark extends from upperparts on to sides of breast. Face white contrasting with dark crown and black patch behind eye. In flight long yellow legs project well behind tail or dangle below the body.
Flight: The wings are held rather stiffly. Dances and jumps over the waves with feet hanging down.
Distribution: A few records within the islands and a few others just outside. Nest on the Kermadec Islands, islands off New Zealand and Australia, also in the Atlantic.

WHITE-BELLIED STORM PETREL *Fregetta grallaria*

Identification: 1. 8″. Head, neck and wings very dark sooty grey, rest of upperparts grey-black except for conspicuous white rump patch. Upperbreast very dark sooty grey and the rest of the underparts white. Tail square-ended.

Distribution: Three records. Breeds on islands in the southern oceans, nearest being the Juan Fernandez group.

White-bellied Storm Petrel

BAND-RUMPED (MADEIRAN) STORM PETREL   pl. 1
Oceanodroma castro

Identification: 1. 8″, w.s. 12″. Largest and most heavily built of the resident storm petrels but still a small bird. All-black except for complete square white patch on rump. Legs and feet do not project behind the slightly forked tail.

Flight: Variable but generally intermediate between the erratic flight of Leach's and the fluttery flight of White-vented Storm Petrel. Less erratic than that of the Wedge-rumped but it is doubtful if Band-rumped Storm Petrel can be identified on flight characters alone. Not seen to follow ships in the area.

Voice: Aerial call at night is a loud, squeaky 'wheekar-wheekar' — like the noise made by rubbing a wet finger on glass. In burrows, displaying birds often churr and utter an occasional 'chica'.

Food: Small fish and cephalopods.

Breeding: Colonial. Single white egg laid in a hole in a sea-cliff or under a boulder. There are two laying periods a year, November-January and May-June, but each pair breeds only once, and at the same season, every year. Nocturnal at breeding areas.

Distribution: Nests on many small islands where there are suitable boulder areas, presence often only indicated by remains of birds killed by Short-eared Owls. Also breeds Hawaii, Japan and several Atlantic islands. Rarely recorded at sea within the islands, due to difficulties of identification and its pelagic feeding habits. Comes aboard boats at night.

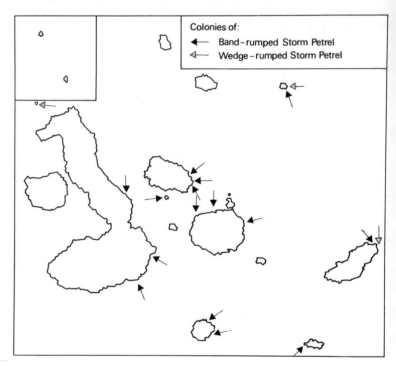

Colonies of:
◄— Band-rumped Storm Petrel
◁— Wedge-rumped Storm Petrel

LEACH'S STORM PETREL *Oceanodroma leucorhoa*   pl. 1

Identification: 1. 8″. All-black except for white rump patch. Tail slightly forked and feet do not project behind tail. All but impossible to distinguish from Band-rumped Storm Petrel, but in the hand Leach's usually has central feathers of white rump dusky.

Flight: Rapid, rather bounding and erratic. Short glides interspaced with rapid wing beats.

Distribution: Few records but probably overlooked due to difficulties of identification. Breeds widely in northern oceans and migrates southwards.

WEDGE-RUMPED (GALAPAGOS) STORM PETREL pl.1
Oceanodroma tethys

Identification: 1. 7", w.s. 10". Similarly plumaged, though smaller and slimmer than the Band-rumped and Leach's Storm Petrels. Rump patch much larger and wedge-shaped with the apex of the white almost reaching notch in slightly forked tail. Each of the white feathers of the rump patch has a thin dark line on shaft.

Flight: More twisting and erratic than the Band-rumped Storm Petrel and less buoyant than that of Leach's Storm Petrel. When feeding may patter or 'walk-on-the-water' but this is more typical of White-vented Storm Petrel.

Breeding: Colonial. Single white egg laid in a hole under the lava or, on Isla Pitt, under a bush. Most eggs laid May-June but birds always present at the colony on Tower. Birds nesting on Isla Pitt vacate the colony between nesting periods. Unique among storm petrels in being diurnal at the breeding colonies.

Food: Very small fish, cephalopods and planktonic crustacea caught mainly at night. Also feeds on fish scraps.

Distribution: Nests on Tower (some 200,000 pairs), Isla Pitt and almost certainly Roca Redonda. Very common at sea. Endemic to the Humboldt Current. Another race breeds in Peru. Map page 62.

BLACK STORM PETREL *Oceanodroma melania*

Identification: 1. 9". All-dark, upper parts sooty-black, underparts brownish black. Often follows ships.

Flight: Tends to be more level and direct than Markham's Storm Petrel.

Distribution: Two records within the islands, common off Ecuadorian mainland. Breeds on Californian islands, migrates to Peru.

Plate 1

SEABIRDS 1

1. **Waved Albatross** *Diomedea irrorata*   53
   Very large. White foreparts; large yellow bill
   a, Head
   b, In flight (not to scale with rest of plate)

2. **Hawaiian Petrel** *Pterodroma phaeopygia*   56
   Large. Black and white; white forehead and sides to tail

3. **Audubon's Shearwater** *Puffinus lherminieri*   59
   Smaller than **2.** Capped appearance
   a, Upperside
   b, Underside

4. **Band-rumped Storm Petrel** *Oceanodroma castro*   61
   Square white rump patch. Tail slightly forked

5. **Leach's Storm Petrel** *Oceanodroma leucorhoa*   62
   Usually a few dark feathers in centre of rump. Tail slightly more
   forked than **4**

6. **Wedge-rumped Storm Petrel** *Oceanodroma tethys*   63
   Triangular white rump patch

7. **White-vented Storm Petrel** *Oceanites gracilis*   60
   Square rump patch, pale centre of belly. Feet project behind tail
   a, Upperside
   b, Underside

8. **White-faced Storm Petrel** *Pelagodroma marina*   60
   Dark grey and white. Very long, yellow legs

Plate 2

SEABIRDS 2

1. **Masked Booby** *Sula dactylatra*   71
  a, Adult: black wing tips and edge to tail
  b, Immature: white extends well up throat

2. **Blue-footed Booby** *Sula nebouxii*   70
  a, Adult: white patches on back and rump; blue feet
  b, Immature: brown bib; feet drab

3. **Red-footed Booby** *Sula sula*   72
  a, Adult: white phase: red feet, blue bill. Sits in trees
  b, Adult: brown phase: red feet, blue bill
  c, Immature: brown with trace of dark breast band; legs, feet and bill dark

4. **Red-billed Tropicbird** *Phaethon aethereus*   67
  Very long central tail feathers

5. **Great Frigatebird** *Fregata minor*   76
  a, Male: green sheen
  b, Female: white extends right up to chin; red eye-ring
  c, Juvenile: white tinged rust, but lacking or less clear in later immatures

6. **Magnificent Frigatebird** *Fregata magnificens*   77
  a, Male: purple sheen
  b, Female: black bib, eye-ring blue
  Juvenile (not illustrated) similar to **5c** but has no rust tinge to white

MARKHAM'S (SOOTY) STORM PETREL
Oceanodroma markhami

Identification: 1. 9.5″. Normally appears totally black but is sooty brown above, slightly paler below. Tail forked. Field identification from Black Storm Petrel is probably impossible though the legs and feet are longer in the Black Storm Petrel. Does not follow ships.

Flight: Rather slow wing beats. Birds rise several feet above water and then sail for a short distance.

Distribution: Two definite records but several all-black storm petrels seen in islands and between Galapagos and Ecuador. Nesting areas unknown but species endemic to the Humboldt Current.

Markham's Storm Petrel

PHAETHONTIDAE: Tropicbirds

RED-BILLED TROPICBIRD *Phaethon aethereus*

Local names Rabijunco, Contramaestre, Piloto

Identification: 1. 39″ including 14-20″ of tail streamers, w.s. 40″. Stockily built, mainly white bird with relatively short wings and with the two central tail feathers greatly elongated and very thin. White plumage marked by black line through the eye, black band on edge of wing and black barrings on upperparts. Bill coral-red in adults, pale yellow in juveniles. Four toes joined by webs.

Flight: Strong and direct with almost constant flapping. In display birds will glide with wings either raised or lowered. Often approaches and circles boats.

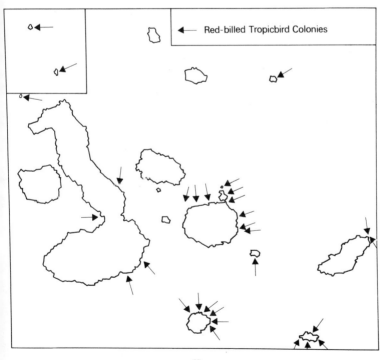

Red-billed Tropicbird Colonies

Voice: A shrill, penetrating 'kree-kree-kree'.

Breeding: Colonial. Single reddish brown, speckled egg laid in hole in a sea cliff or rock pile. In most large colonies breeding occurs throughout the year but the population on Plaza Island has an annual breeding cycle with eggs laid August-February. Dead and starving young are frequently found at colonies. Breeds in fifth year, at least 82% of adults survive from one year to the next.

Food: Fish and squid caught by diving from flight. Normally feeds well away from land.

Distribution: Nests on seacliffs and smaller islets throughout the archipelago, though less common in the colder waters around Fernandina and western Isabela. Birds ringed in Galapagos have been recorded off Panama and Peru. The species is widespread in the tropics. Not infrequently comes aboard ships at night.

Note: Records of Yellow-billed Tropicbird *P. lepturus* almost certainly refer to juvenile Red-billed Tropicbirds.

Juvenile Red-billed Tropicbird

PELECANIDAE: Pelicans

BROWN PELICAN *Pelecanus occidentalis*
Local names Pelicano café, Alcatras.

Identification: 1. 4′, w.s. 6-7′. Unmistakable due to large size and characteristic bill. Adult mainly brown, with striking chestnut and white markings on head and neck when in breeding plumage. Immature lacks these markings and is paler beneath. Four toes joined by webs.

Flight: Normally a few rapid wing beats followed by glide. Birds will fly in orderly rows, flapping and gliding in unison. Often circles in thermals. Note the splayed wing tips.

Voice: Normally silent but young hiss and clap bills.

Food: Fish caught by diving from the air. Will also feed on waste from fishing boats and attack birds to pirate food.

Breeding: Nests in small colonies in mangroves or other lower bushes, rarely on the ground. Two or three chalky-white eggs laid on a flimsy platform of twigs. Breeding occurs at all times of year but pairs within a colony nest synchronously and have peaks of breeding at less than yearly intervals. Very successful in raising young but many immatures die soon after fledging when they have difficulty in mastering the specialised fishing technique.

Distribution: Common breeder on all the main central islands; also nests on Marchena and Hood. Uncommon visitor to Tower, Pinta and Wenman, unrecorded on Culpepper. Widespread in the Americas and West Indies.

Adult Brown Pelican

SULIDAE: Boobies and gannets

BLUE-FOOTED BOOBY *Sula nebouxii*   page 73 and **pl. 2**
Local name Piquero patas azules
Identification: 1. 29-35", w.s. 5'. The commonest and most nondescript of
Galapagos boobies. Adults have head and neck white mottled with brown,
upperparts brown except for diagnostic white patches on mantle and rump,
and underparts white. Feet and legs bright blue. Immature darker with
brown head and neck, more white on mantle and back of neck, lacks white
on the rump; brown on the neck forms a distinct bib on upper breast.
Immature Masked Boobies always have centre of throat white. Immatures
have grey feet and legs. Female larger than male and appears to have a
larger dark pupil in eye contrasting with yellow iris; this is due to dark
pigment around the pupil and not to any difference in size. The sexual eye
difference does not apply to immatures. All boobies have webs between
the four toes.
Flight: Direct, several flaps followed by a glide. When hunting birds fly
with bill pointing downwards.
Voice: Adult males have a plaintive whistle, adult females and immatures a
hoarse, duck-like note.
Food: Fish caught by plunge-diving, often into very shallow water.
Breeding: Colonial. Two or three chalky white eggs laid on the ground. In
large colonies there is almost continuous breeding and pairs may nest every
seven to nine months. Birds may desert small colonies between breeding
periods. First breeds when three years old.
Distribution: Breeds on most islands except those north of the equator.
Has bred Tower. Three young ringed in Galapagos have been reported
from the mainland of Ecuador. Occurs from western Mexico to north
Peru.

MASKED (WHITE) BOOBY *Sula dactylatra*   page 73 and **pl. 2**

Local names Piquero patas verdes, Piquero blanco

Identification: 1. 30-35", w.s. 5-6'. The largest booby. Adult unlikely to be mistaken due to dazzling white plumage broken only by very dark brown, almost black, band on outer and rear edges of wings, and dark brown edge to tail. Bill pink or yellow with surrounding area of bare skin blue-black, feet grey or greeny. Immature grey-brown above and superficially similar to immature Blue-footed Booby but white of underparts extends well up centre of throat, and also around on to back of neck. When seen head-on in flight, dark of head is separate from dark of body and wings. The immature has been mistaken for the Brown Booby *S. leucogaster* but this species has a sharp demarcation between the dark brown upper breast and white underparts.

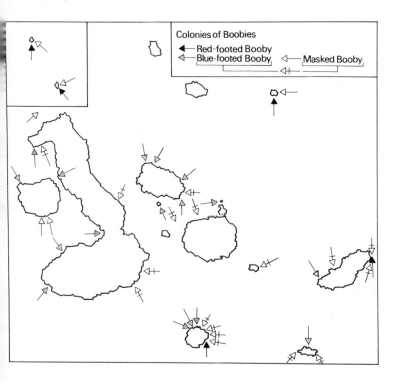

Flight: Direct and rapid, alternately flapping and gliding.

Voice: Males whistle, females trumpet.

Food: Fish caught by diving from the air. Normally feeds near or between the islands, rarely inshore.

Breeding: Colonial on cliffs or near sea-edge. Two chalky white eggs laid on ground but only a single young survives more than a few days. The only Galapagos sulid with an annual breeding cycle but nesting is out of phase on different islands; most eggs on Tower laid August to November, on Hood November to February. First breeds when three years old. At least 87% of adults survive from one year to the next.

Distribution: Common on most islands and often roosts on islands where does not nest. Widespread in the tropics and subtropics.

BROWN BOOBY *Sula leucogaster*

Identification: l. 30″, w.s. 5′. A fairly large booby. Adult has upperparts, head, neck and upper breast dark brown, sharply demarcated from white lower breast, remaining underparts and underwings. Immatures dull brown, lighter where adult is white but the demarcation is still obvious and separates them from the paler young Red-footed Booby. Adult bill yellow.

Distribution: Single definite record of an adult but most probable sightings can safely be attributed to mis-identified young Masked Boobies. Common throughout the tropics, including seas between Galapagos and Panama.

RED-FOOTED BOOBY *Sula sula*   pl.2

Local name Piquero patas rojas

Identification: l. 29″, w.s. 4.5′. Two colour phases. In Galapagos most adults are all brown except for red legs and feet and light blue bill with red base. About 5% of breeding birds resemble Masked Boobies but are smaller with far less black on wings; feet and legs red, bill blue. Intermediates occur with white patches on wings, tail and rump. Immature all brown with an indistinct narrow dark band across the breast; legs, feet and bill dark.

Flight: Appears more graceful than other boobies and birds sometimes shear the waves like shearwaters.

Food: Fish caught by diving or, sometimes in the case of flying fish, caught in flight between waves. Feeds well away from the breeding colonies.

Breeding: Colonial. Single chalky white egg laid on a frail platform of twigs in a bush or low tree. Eggs found all months but breeding within a colony is synchronised, probably by availability of food.

Distribution: Breeds on Tower (about 140,000 pairs), Culpepper, Wenman, Gardner-near-Floreana, Punta and Isla Pitt. Rarely seen ashore where does not breed, e.g. Hood, Seymour, Roca Redonda, Gordon Rocks east of Plaza. Only infrequently noted at sea within the archipelago away from the breeding grounds. Widespread in tropical oceans. Map page 71.

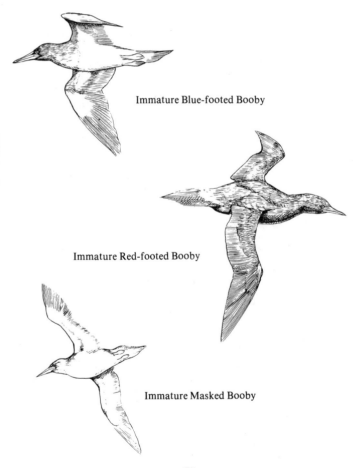

Immature Blue-footed Booby

Immature Red-footed Booby

Immature Masked Booby

PHALACROCORACIDAE: Cormorants

FLIGHTLESS CORMORANT *Nannopterum harrisi*
Local names Cormoran, Pato cuervo
Identification: 1. 35″. Unmistakable, large dark bird with apparently functionless, tatty wings. Adults almost black above, brownish below, turquoise eye. Juveniles glossy black all over with dull coloured eye. Bill long, strong with a hooked tip; legs and feet sturdy and dark. Stiff tail. All four toes joined by webs. Male noticeably larger than female. Often seen on the tide-edge 'drying' wings. Swims very low in water using feet for propulsion. The breast bone or sternum has lost the keel which in most birds serves as attachment for flight muscles.
Food: Bottom-living fish, eels and octopuses.
Voice: Adults make a low growl, young a plaintive 'wee-wee'.

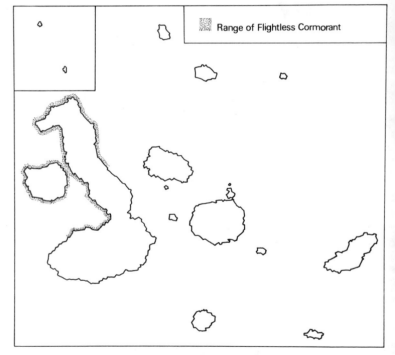

Breeding: Nest in very small colonies on sheltered boulder beaches, rocks and lagoons. Two or three whitish eggs laid in bulky nest of seaweed built just above high-water mark. Most eggs laid March to September but pairs may be found breeding at any time. Nesting success is very low. Some birds nest more than once a year. Young fed by both parents for some time after they take to the water, then only by the male while the female may breed again, with another male. This is one of the few seabirds which does not retain the same mate from one nesting to the next. First breeds when two years old. About 87% of adults survive from one year to the next.

Distribution: Breeds in suitable areas around the coasts of Fernandina and Isabela (except the southern and south-eastern parts from Punta Garcia to Punta Moreno). Only record outside breeding range is at Caleta Webb. Endemic, population about 800 pairs.

Flightless Cormorant

FREGATIDAE: Frigatebirds

GREAT FRIGATEBIRD *Fregata minor*   pl. 2

Local names for frigatebirds Fragata, Tijereta.

Identification: 1. 40″, w.s. 7.5′, weight 2.3 lb. Male all-black with blue-green sheen on head and back, and brown band across the medium wing coverts. Wings long and pointed, tail long and very deeply forked. Males in breeding condition have a red, distensible throat pouch inflated during courtship. Female black above save for paler band on wings; breast and upper belly white with the white extending up to chin. Juveniles have upperparts brownish black, underparts, head and neck white, usually tinged with rust. Several intermediate plumages between juvenile and adult. Adults have fleshy ring around the eye which is reddish in female, blue in male.

Flight: Frigatebirds spend long periods circling and gliding, and when forced to flap do so with deep, slow wing beats. Normal flight gives no indication of the great manoeuvrability and speed shown when chasing other seabirds or picking food from surface of water. Very high wing area in relation to weight.

Voice: Near food or before landing a rapid series of 'tchuk-tchuk . . .'.

Breeding: Colonial. Single white egg laid on a platform of twigs in tree or bush. An annual breeder but season varies from island to island. On Tower most eggs laid February to August whereas peak of laying on Hood is April to November. Rearing a chick takes so long that successful breeders can not nest every year.

Food: Fish, picked from surface of sea or by forcing other seabirds to disgorge their last feeds; also young and eggs of seabirds, young turtles, fish waste.

Distribution: Widely scattered breeder throughout the archipelago with main colonies on Tower, Culpepper, Wenman, Hood, Gardner-near-Floreana, Tortuga Island, Crossman Islands, Seymour, Isla and Punta Pitt. Widespread in tropical ocean.

MAGNIFICENT FRIGATEBIRD *Fregata magnificens*   pl. 2

Identification: 1. 42″, w.s. 7.5′. Adult male almost indistinguishable from Great Frigatebird but upperparts have a metallic purple sheen and wings lack brown band. Female is distinguished by having white underparts with a conspicuous black throat patch. Immatures have white parts without rusty coloration. Eye-ring blue in both sexes.

Food: Fish, chiefly caught directly and less often by cleptoparasitism. Also eats offal and fish waste so is the species normally seen around man's activities.

Breeding: Colonial. Single white egg laid on a platform of twigs in tree, bush or cactus. Prolonged laying period but most eggs laid June-August. Young fed by both sexes for three months, then just by the female for eight months or more.

Distribution: Main breeding colonies on Seymour, Wenman, Culpepper, Punta Moreno (Isabela), Wreck Bay (San Cristóbal) and Kicker Rock. Often a few pairs in colonies of Great Frigatebirds, e.g. Tower, Tortuga Island. Elsewhere widespread near coast of tropical America, West Indies and Cape Verde Islands. Birds ringed at Wreck Bay have been recovered in Costa Rica and Colombia.

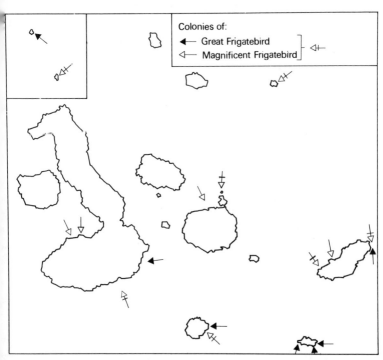

Colonies of:
◀— Great Frigatebird
◁— Magnificent Frigatebird

ARDEIDAE: Herons

GREAT BLUE HERON *Ardea herodias*   pl.5

Local name Garza morena

Identification: 1. 4.5', w.s. 6.5'. By far the largest heron in islands. Mostly grey with black and white on head and streaked breast. At rest shows black and rufous on bend of folded wing. Immatures have more brown markings on wing and lack the black and white head plumes of adults. Dagger shaped bill yellow, very long legs and feet grey.

Flight: Wing beats are slow and deliberate. Normally flies with head drawn back on to shoulders.

Voice: Normally silent but if disturbed may utter a loud 'kraak'.

Food: Mainly fish caught at the tide edge; lizards, young marine iguanas and young birds.

Breeding: Usually a solitary nester but up to six nests recorded together near favourable feeding areas. Two or three bluish eggs laid on a platform of twigs, usually in mangroves. Breeding throughout year.

Distribution: Restricted to the coastal areas of all the main islands, though rare on Hood and Tower, and apparently unrecorded on the four most northern islands. Breeds in North and Central America, replaced by the closely related White-necked Heron *Ardea cocoi* in South America.

Immature Great Blue Heron

COMMON EGRET *Casmerodius albus* pl.5

Local name Garza blanca

Identification: 1. 40″, w.s. 4.5′, b. 4.5″. A large, slender all-white heron with powerful yellow bill. Far larger, and commoner, than other white herons and the only one with black legs and feet. In full breeding plumage has fine plumes extending down back.

Flight: Slow and deliberate with deep wing beats. At a distance may be mistaken for Swallow-tailed Gull. As with other herons, the head is drawn back and the legs trail behind.

Food: Small fish, lizards, grasshoppers and other insects, small birds. Sometimes visits seabird colonies where often intensively mobbed by the occupants.

Breeding: Few records of nests in mangroves holding no more than two eggs or young.

Distribution: Probably breeds on most of the main central islands but rare on Hood and Pinta, unknown on other outlying islands. Normally restricted to coastal areas, rare inland. Widespread in the world.

SNOWY EGRET *Egretta thula* pl.5

Identification: 1. 25″, w.s. 36″, b. 3.5″. A small, totally white egret with rather slender black bill and yellow lores, black legs and yellow feet. Much smaller than the Common Egret and separated from the Cattle Egret by black (not yellow) bill.

Flight: Slightly more rapid than Common Egret.

Distribution: Uncommon visitor, first recorded in 1965. Since then seen irregularly August to April. Widespread in the Americas.

CATTLE EGRET *Bubulcus ibis* pl. 5

Identification: 1. 20″, w.s. 36″, b. 2.5″. A small white heron with relatively short neck and bill. Plumage all-white except that adults in breeding plumage have buffy tinge to head and back. Bill yellow, legs and feet normally yellow in adults, darker in immatures. The Common Egret also has a yellow bill but is much larger and sleeker. Similar sized Snowy Egret has black beak and legs.

Flight: More rapid than the other white herons, shorter wing beats.

Distribution: Regular visitor July to April. First recorded in 1964 and gradually becoming commoner. Normally seen with cattle in highlands but also with sealions. After a spectacular recent expansion the species is now virtually world wide.

Plate 3

WATERBIRDS AND RAILS

1. **Greater Flamingo** *Phoenicopterus ruber*   84
   Pink. (Head and bill shown to scale with the other birds on this plate)

2. **White-cheeked Pintail** *Anas bahamensis*   85
   Brown cap, white cheeks; green wing speculum

3. **Blue-winged Teal** *Anas discors*   86
   Blue wing patch; green speculum

4. **Pied-billed Grebe** *Podilymbus podiceps*   53
   Chicken-like bill; white undertail

5. **Common Gallinule** *Gallinula chloropus*   89
   a, Adult: white undertail and side stripe; red bill with yellow tip
   b, Immature: brown, trace of side stripe; bill horn

6. **Galapagos Rail** *Laterallus spilonotus*   88
   Very small. Chestnut and white spots on upperparts, dark bill and legs

7. **Paint-billed Crake** *Neocrex erythrops*   88
   Small. All dark; yellow and red bill; red legs

Plate 4

HAWKS AND OWLS

1. **Galapagos Hawk** *Buteo galapagoensis* 86
   a, Adult: mainly dark, yellow bill
   b, Adult: in flight (from below)
   c, Immature: body buff, mottled brown
   Juvenile has breast and belly chestnut

2. **Short-eared Owl** *Asio flammeus* 121
   Round facial disc, short 'ear-tufts'. In flight black patch on bend
   of wing

3. **Osprey** *Pandion haliaetus* 87
   Mainly white underparts with black mark on underwing. In
   flight wings crooked

4. **Barn Owl** *Tyto alba* 121
   Usually very pale, heart-shaped facial disc

5. **Peregrine** *Falco peregrinus* 87
   Dark grey or brown, pointed wings; black moustache, long tail
   a, At rest
   b, In flight

LAVA HERON *Butorides sundevalli* pl. 5

Local name Garza verde

Identification: l. 16", w.s. 25", b. 2.5". Adult is the only small, all-dark heron in the islands. Upperparts dark green, underparts slightly paler. Crown feathers elongated to form crest. Bill dark but feet and legs bright yellow or orange. Immatures brown, heavily streaked darker.

Flight: Direct and purposeful, usually close to water or ground. Feet trail behind the tail showing off the brightly coloured soles of the feet.

Voice: When annoyed or alarmed bird will raise its crest and utter a sharp 'skeow'.

Food: Small fish (caught either by stealth or kingfisher-like diving), lizards, prawns and small crabs.

Breeding: Usually solitary but in optimum feeding areas two or three pairs may nest close together, usually in mangrove thicket or under rocks. One to three green eggs laid in nest of twigs. Nests found all months but most nesting September to March, some pairs breed more than once a year.

Distribution: Common nester on the coasts of all islands. Endemic.

STRIATED HERON *Butorides striatus* pl. 5

Identification: l. 16". A small heron, rather similar to and previously confused with the Lava Heron, but much paler, never all dark. Back of neck and sides of head blue-grey, contrasting with black cap. Back grey and wing coverts green with pale fringes. Underparts grey except for chin, centre of neck and breast which are white or pale buff, streaked dark. Bill dark, legs and feet yellow-orange. Immature paler than the Lava Heron and with far less streaking on underparts. Belly sometimes lacks streaks.

Individuals intermediate between Lava and Striated Herons occur and present knowledge is inconclusive as to whether both species occur and hybridise, or whether there is a single very variable species.

Food: Small crabs, fish.

Breeding: No information.

Distribution: Only recorded from Fernandina, Isabela, Santa Cruz, San Cristóbal, Duncan and Pinta but to be expected elsewhere. Although only recently recognised as being a breeding species, it is not a recent coloniser as skins collected by the 1905-6 Academy Expedition can be assigned to this species.

Note: The taxonomy of this genus is complicated and Lava and Striated Herons might be forms of a single species.

YELLOW-CROWNED NIGHT HERON *Nyctanassa violacea*

Local names Garza nocturna, Huaque **pl. 5**

Identification: 1. 24", w.s. 46", b. 3". A stocky grey heron with large eyes and short, thick black bill. Adults have body grey with black stripings on back and wings. Head black with white patch running from join of the mandibles backward under the eye, and black or yellow crown with long white plumes. The large eye is brown or orange, legs and feet dull. Juvenile is grey-brown, heavily spotted and streaked with white and lacks head markings. Some birds breed in an intermediate plumage with traces of the adult markings but head and mantle brown.

Flight: Strong and direct.

Voice: A series of rapid 'quock'.

Food: Red crabs, some centipedes, scorpions, beetles, etc. caught mainly at night.

Breeding: Solitary. Two to four blue-green eggs laid in nest of twigs placed low in mangrove, thick bush or under a rock. Breeds throughout year.

Distribution: Common nester throughout the islands except Culpepper and Wenman (? overlooked). Commonest in coastal area but does occur inland. Widespread in temperate and tropical America.

BLACK-CROWNED NIGHT HERON *Nycticorax nycticorax*

Identification: 1. 23", w.s. 45", b. 3". Very similar to Yellow-crowned Night Heron but adult more contrastingly black and white. Crown and back are black, wings and tail grey, underparts white. Bill black, legs and feet yellow. Immature is difficult to separate from resident species but the white spots on the basically brown plumage tend to be larger.

Distribution: Single record. Widespread in many parts of the world. Some North American birds are migratory.

PHOENICOPTERIDAE: Flamingos

GREATER FLAMINGO *Phoenicopterus ruber*　　　　　　**pl. 3**

Local name Flamenco

Identification: 1. 4′, w.s. 5′. Unmistakable due to large size, characteristic shape with long curved neck and long legs, and pink to vermilion plumage. Main wing feathers are black. Immatures lack bright coloration. Heavy bill yellow or pinkish with black end. Legs and webbed feet grey or flesh coloured. Male noticeably larger than female.

Flight: Flies with rapid wing beats; head and legs extended.

Voice: Rather goose-like.

Feeding: Crustaceans and other minute animals filtered from the mud and water by the highly specialised bill.

Breeding: Nests in small colonies. Single white egg laid in a depression on top of a mud-pile constructed for this purpose. Breeding occurs whenever water conditions are suitable.

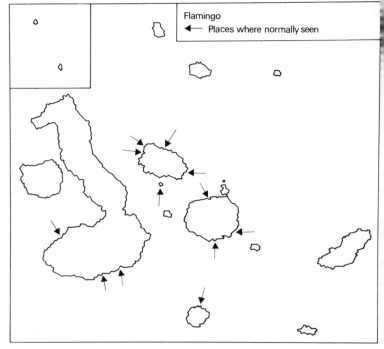

Flamingo
← Places where normally seen

Distribution: Seen regularly, and nests, on a few salt lagoons and pans on James, Bainbridge Rocks, Floreana, Jervis, Santa Cruz and south Isabela. Population 500-1,000 birds. Breeds in many other places in the world.

One of the shyest of Galapagos birds—should never be made to fly or otherwise disturbed.

ANATIDAE: Ducks

BLACK-BELLIED TREE DUCK *Dendrocygna autumnalis*
Identification: 1. 21″. A long legged, long necked, rather gooselike duck. Breast, neck and back brown, sides and belly are black. Large white areas on the wings. Legs and bill pink.
Flight: Slow wing beats; head and feet hang slightly down.
Distribution: Single record of the southern race which occurs in the Guayas basin and northwards to eastern Panama.

Black-bellied Tree Duck

WHITE-CHEEKED PINTAIL *Anas bahamensis*   **pl. 3**
Local name Patillo
Identification: 1. 12″. The only common duck in the islands. Body brown, feathers of the upperparts tinged grey, those of underparts spotted dark brown. Top of head brown but throat and cheeks white, giving the bird a capped appearance. Conspicuous iridescent green wing patch or speculum, widely bordered with buff. Bill dark with pink or reddish base.
Flight: Take off almost vertically upwards; rapid, shallow wing beats.
Food: Vegetable matter, some invertebrates picked from the surface of the water or by up-ending. Birds normally dive only to escape predators.
Breeding: Up to ten pale brown eggs laid in nest lined with down made in dense vegetation near water. Breeds whenever conditions are suitable.

Distribution: Occurs on all the main islands where there are salt lagoons, temporary or permanent freshwater. Rare on the sea. Also breeds in the West Indies and South America. The distinct Galapagos race was once described as a separate species.

BLUE-WINGED TEAL *Anas discors* pl. 3

Identification: 1. 15″. A small brownish duck with conspicuous large, pale blue patch on shoulder which is obvious in flight. At rest this patch sometimes shows as a horizontal blue line. Green wing speculum. Adult male has white crescent in front of eye and white patch on the flanks, black around tail. Immediately told from the resident species by the blue wing patch.

Distribution: Regular visitor in small numbers. Recorded most months but commonest October to March, usually on inland freshwater ponds, less commonly on coastal lagoons. Nests in North America and migrates to most of South America.

Wing of Blue-winged Teal

ACCIPITRIDAE: Hawks

GALAPAGOS HAWK *Buteo galapagoensis* pl.4

Local name Gavilán

Identification: 1. 22″, w.s. 4′. The only large and dark, broad winged bird likely to be seen sitting in a tree or circling high in the sky. Adult almost black except for some chestnut on underparts and a grey or brown tail crossed by about nine darker bands. Immature has body buff coloured, mottled with dark brown. Recently fledged juveniles have breast and belly bright chestnut. Bill dark with yellow cere or fleshy base, legs and feet yellow. Female larger than male.

Flight: In calm conditions alternates periods of flapping with long glides. Sometimes hovers.

Voice: Common call is loud 'kee-kee-kee-kee...'.

Food: Wide variety of sea- and land-birds (especially doves, finches), native and introduced rats, lizards, iguanas, invertebrates (especially centipedes) and carrion.

Breeding: Territorial. Two or three white eggs, sometimes speckled brown, laid in a large nest of twigs on rock outcrop or in tree. Breeding occurs all months but a peak May to July. Often two or more males mated with each female, all of which help to raise the young.

Care should be taken when entering territories as birds with eggs or young are well able to defend them from human intruders.

Distribution: Previously common on all main islands except Tower, Culpepper and Wenman. Now extinct on Floreana, San Cristóbal, Seymour, Baltra and Daphne, and very much reduced on Santa Cruz due to human interference and killing. Total population about 130 pairs. Endemic.

PANDIONIDAE: Osprey

OSPREY *Pandion haliaetus* **pl. 4**

Identification: 1. 22″, w.s. 4.5′. A large hawk normally seen circling overhead. Upperparts dark brown, underparts largely white; underwing mottled light and dark with a conspicuous black patch on the bend of the wing. Head largely white with black mark through eye and down side of neck. Distinguished from Galapagos Hawk by mainly white body and black mark on underwing.

Flight: A conspicuous crook in the leading edge of the wing, and the wings bow downwards.

Food: Fish caught by diving feet first into the water.

Distribution: An annual visitor in very small numbers during the northern winter. An occasional bird oversummers. Species widespread; North American birds migrate south.

FALCONIDAE: Falcons

PEREGRINE FALCON *Falco peregrinus* **pl. 4**

Identification: 1. 15-20″, w.s. 40-45″. A strong, pigeon-shaped, hawk with pointed wings and long tail. Adult grey above, white or buff below, lightly spotted on upper breast and belly. Immature brown above, heavily streaked dark below. Conspicuous black moustache.

Flight: Direct and very fast; dives at speed onto prey.

Food: Recorded diving at Blue-footed Boobies, tropicbirds, Lava Gulls and shorebirds. Also eats finches.

Distribution: Regular visitor in very small numbers. Most records November to March but also May-June. Widespread species, northern breeding birds migrate south, southern birds migrate north.

RALLIDAE:Rails and crakes

GALAPAGOS RAIL *Laterallus spilonotus* pl. 3
Local name Pachay

Identification: 1. 6″. A very small, very secretive but remarkably tame rail. All dark except for some chestnut on upperparts and white dots on wings. Paint-billed Crake lacks chestnut and the spots. Legs, feet and bill dark.

Flight: Loath to fly—invariably escapes by running.

Voice: 'Kick-kick-keh-kah'.

Food: Invertebrates and some seeds picked from the soil and leaf litter.

Breeding: Up to six eggs, cream with fine speckling, laid in nest in isolated clump of vegetation. Breeding recorded September to April.

Distribution: Common in the highlands of Santa Cruz, James and formerly Pinta. Also recorded from Isabela, Fernandina, Floreana, San Cristóbal, and Baltra. Usually seen in the damp highlands, in earlier times also in mangrove areas. Endemic.

PAINT-BILLED CRAKE *Neocrex erythrops* pl. 3
Local name Gallareta

Identification: 1. 8″. Small, all-dark crake with yellow bill with red base. Red legs. Although very secretive more often seen than Galapagos Rail and identifiable by its all dark plumage and red bill.

Flight: Weak-looking with rapid wing beats and dangling feet. Will fly if disturbed but lands in the first available cover.

Voice: Alarm call is a sharp 'twak'. When feeding calls 'tchur-ur-ur-oo'.

Food: Invertebrates from soil and leaf litter.

Breeding: Up to seven pale cream eggs, heavily blotched red-brown, laid in a nest of grass in a clump of vegetation. Main laying period December to February.

Distribution: Only recorded since 1953, breeds on Santa Cruz, Floreana, San Cristóbal, Isabela (Alcedo), recorded Tower (once). Could occur elsewhere. Commonest in and just below the farmlands on Santa Cruz. Breeds in northern parts of South America.

SORA RAIL *Porzana carolina*

Identification: 1. 7″. Small, plump rail, grey-brown with black patch on face and (adult) throat. Bill yellow.

Distribution: Single birds found dead on Marchena, James and Tower. Nests in North America, winters south to Peru.

COMMON GALLINULE (MOORHEN) *Gallinula chloropus*

Local name Gallinula **pl. 3**

Identification: 1. 14″. A sooty black waterbird with prominent white patch under tail, band of white feathers along sides of body, bright red bill with yellow tip and red frontal head plate. Long yellow legs. Immatures brown with horn coloured bill. Normally seen swimming when head is characteristically pumped back and forth.

Flight: When disturbed flies rather feebly with the long legs dangling. Often escapes by diving.

Voice: Chicken-like 'cluck'.

Food: Vegetable matter and invertebrates found at the water's edge or by diving.

Breeding: Little information.

Distribution: Confined to a few areas of brackish water and inland ponds on San Cristóbal, Santa Cruz, Floreana, Fernandina (possibly not resident) and southern Isabela. Recorded once on Barrington. Found throughout the world.

PURPLE GALLINULE *Porphyrula martinica*

Identification: 12″. Superficially similar to resident Gallinule. Adult has head and upperparts dark blue, back brownish or green. Bill red with yellow tip, frontal shield blue, legs and feet yellow. Lacks the white line along body. Immature has upperparts rich brown, wings with greenish tinge, underparts buff or white.

Distribution: Three records in islands, another between Galapagos and continent. Breeds in temperate and tropical Americas.

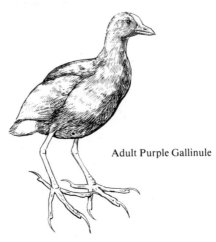

Adult Purple Gallinule

HAEMATOPODIDAE: Oystercatchers

OYSTERCATCHER *Haematopus palliatus* pl.9

Local names Ostrero, Cangrejero

Identification: 1. 18″, b. 3.5″. Large tame, black and white shorebird with long, relatively stout red bill, flesh-coloured feet and legs. Upperparts, head and breast black, underparts white. In flight shows white stripe on inner part of wing and some white at base of tail. Eye yellow. Immature has dark tip to bill.

Flight: Rapid and direct with rather short and quick wing beats. In display flight, wing beats are exaggerated and flight butterfly-like.

Voice: Loud and shrill 'kleep', repeated rapidly.

Food: Intertidal invertebrates, especially molluscs, sea-urchins, crabs.

Breeding: Territorial. Two buff speckled eggs laid in a scrape just above the high tide level. Young leave the nest immediately after hatching. Most nests October to March.

Distribution: Isolated pairs found on coasts of the main islands. The total population is possibly less than 100 pairs—due to restricted suitable feeding areas.

Oystercatcher

CHARADRIIDAE: Plovers

BLACK-BELLIED (GREY) PLOVER *Squatarola squatarola*

pl. 10

Identification: 1. 11″, b. 1.2″. A medium-sized and upright standing wader. In winter plumage upperparts are grey-brown speckled with white, underparts paler and belly almost white. In breeding plumage (uncommon) face, neck and breast are black. Diagnostic black patch under the wings where they join body. In flight shows a white wing bar and rump patch. Short, stout bill and legs black.

Voice: Three-syllabic whistle.

Distribution: Regular migrant in small numbers. Recorded in all months but commonest during the northern winter. Prefers sand beaches. A circumpolar breeding species which migrates south as far as Chile.

GOLDEN PLOVER *Pluvialis dominica*

Identification: 1. 10″, b. 0.9″. Very similar to the Grey Plover but lacks wing bar, rump patch and black underwing patch. Upperparts more brown but still speckled with white.

Voice: A whistled 'quee' or 'queedle'.

Distribution: Three records. Breeds in North America and Asia, a migrant to South America.

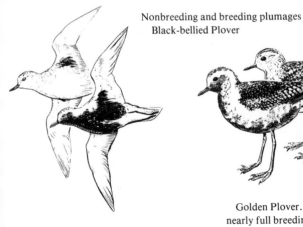

Nonbreeding and breeding plumages
Black-bellied Plover

Golden Plover. Adult in
nearly full breeding plumage
(left) and immature plumage (right)

SEMIPALMATED PLOVER *Charadrius semipalmatus* pl.10

Identification: 1.7″, b. 0.6″. A small dumpy shorebird, brownish above except for white collar, white forehead and stripe above eye. Underparts white except for brown band across chest. In adult plumage head and breast markings are black instead of brown. Bill dark with orange base (adults) or all dark (immatures); legs orange-yellow. In flight shows pale wing bar and sides to tail. When disturbed characteristically runs a few steps, then stops, before running off again.

Voice: A plaintive 'chi-we'.

Distribution: Common migrant between August and April, small numbers present throughout the year. Commonest on sandy beaches, rarely occurs in the highlands. Breeds in Arctic America, a migrant to most of South America.

THICK-BILLED PLOVER *Charadrius wilsonia*

Identification: 1. 7″, b. 0.8″. Similar to Semipalmated Plover but bill longer and heavier and coloured black. Legs and feet flesh or grey coloured.

Voice: A whistled 'wheet'.

Distribution: Single record. Breeds in North and South America, northern birds migrate to South America.

Semipalmated Plover

Thick-billed Plover

KILLDEER *Charadrius vociferus*

Identification: l. 10″, b. 0.7″. Much larger than two previous species with two (not one) breast bands and a longer, wedge-shaped tail. Tail and lower back bright rufous or orange. Bill black, feet and legs flesh-coloured. In flight shows wing bar and white edgings to the tail.

Voice: An attention-drawing 'killdeer' or 'deee'.

Distribution: A few records. Birds breeding in North America migrate south, also nests Peru and Chile.

RUDDY TURNSTONE *Arenaria interpres*   pl. 10

Identification: l. 9″, b. 0.9″. A small, robust shorebird of rocky coasts. In breeding plumage unmistakable with russet on back, white and black patterned head and breast; rest of underparts white. In other plumages back and head brown or grey, underparts white with a suggestion of dark breast patch. Chin and upper throat always white. In flight upperparts a harlequin pattern of black, white and rufous. Two wing bars and tail white with broad subterminal black band. Timing of attainment of breeding dress very variable and a whole range of plumages may be seen in a single flock. Black bill stout and slightly upturned. Legs orange.

Voice: A sharp and hard 'tuk-a-tuk'.

Distribution: A very common species always to be found on rocky shores, also on sand beaches, salt lagoons and inland. Most numerous August to March. A circumpolar species in the northern hemisphere. Migrant in South America.

Ruddy Turnstone in
breeding plumage

BLACK TURNSTONE *Arenaria melanocephala*

Identification: 1. 9", b. 0.9". Very similar to Ruddy Turnstone but lacks red and brown in plumage. Chin always dark. Legs and feet usually black, rarely dusky red.

Voice: Higher pitched than Ruddy Turnstone.

Distribution: Two records. Breeds Alaska and migrates southwards.

Black Turnstone

SURFBIRD *Aphriza virgata* **pl. 10**

Identification: 1. 10", b. 1". Similarly shaped to Ruddy Turnstone, but noticeably larger. In non-breeding plumage upperparts grey-brown, breast grey, belly white with dark markings. In breeding plumage upperparts mottled with black and chestnut, underparts heavily spotted dark. Bill yellow with black tip, feet and legs yellow. In flight shows conspicuous white wing bar and white tail with black triangle at tip.

Voice: A plaintive three-note whistle.

Distribution: Rare migrant September to March, possibly overlooked in flocks of Ruddy Turnstone. Breeds Alaska and migrates as far as southern Chile.

Surfbird

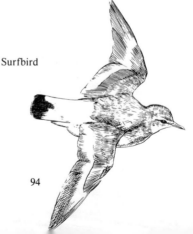

SCOLOPACIDAE: Sandpipers

SOLITARY SANDPIPER *Tringa solitaria*   **pl. 9**

Identification: 1. 8", b. 1.3". Superficially like commoner Lesser Yellow-legs but smaller and with dark rump and legs. Upperparts mainly dark with few spots, underparts white with few streaks on sides of breast. White ring around eye. Bill dark and relatively long. In flight no wing bar or rump patch but distinctive barred black and white sides to tail. Underwing coverts dark.

Voice: 'Peet-weet-weet', higher than Spotted Sandpiper.

Distribution: Rare visitor in some northern winters. Most records from the highlands of Santa Cruz. Breeds Alaska and Canada, migrates to the Andes and eastern South America.

Solitary Sandpiper

Plate 5

HERONS AND EGRETS

1. **Great Blue Heron** *Ardea herodias*   78
   Large. Dagger-shaped bill

2. **Yellow-crowned Night Heron** *Nyctanassa violacea*   83
   a, Adult: medium-sized grey body; black and white head
   markings
   b, Immature: grey-brown, heavily spotted white

3. **Striated Heron** *Butorides striatus*   82
   Small. Centre of breast and neck pale with dark streakings;
   black cap

4. **Lava Heron** *Butorides sundevalli*   82
   Small
   a, Adult: all dark
   b, Immature: brown, heavily streaked

5. **Common Egret** *Casmerodius albus*   79
   Large. Bill yellow; feet and legs black

6. **Cattle Egret** *Bubulcus ibis*   79
   Small. Bill yellow; legs and feet yellow or pink

7. **Snowy Egret** *Egretta thula*   79
   Small. Bill and legs black, feet yellow

Plate 6

MOCKINGBIRDS, DOVE, CUCKOO, FLYCATCHERS

-4. Mockingbirds *Nesomimus species*

Thrush-like birds with longish bills and long tails, each feather with pale tip. Species depends on island

1. Galapagos Mockingbird *N. parvulus* on most islands	126
2. Hood Mockingbird *N. macdonaldi* on Hood	128
3. Chatham Mockingbird *N. melanotis* on San Cristóbal	128
4. Charles Mockingbird *N. trifasciatus* on Gardner-near-Floreana and Champion	128

5. Galapagos Dove *Zenaida galapagoensis*   119

Mantle feathers and wing coverts black and white; blue eye ring; red legs.

6. Dark-billed Cuckoo *Coccyzus melacoryphus*   120

Much rufous; grey crown

7. Large-billed Flycatcher *Myiarchus magnirostris*   123

Sulphur belly; throat and breast grey

8. Vermilion Flycatcher *Pyrocephalus rubinus*   123

a, **Adult male: vermillion underparts**
b, **Immature male: pinkish underparts**
c, **Female: bright yellow underparts**

LESSER YELLOWLEGS *Totanus flavipes*   pl. 9

Identification: 1. 10″, b. 1.5″. A medium-sized, long legged and rather elongated looking wader. Upperparts grey brown spotted with white, neck and breast paler grey, belly white. Pale eye stripe. Relatively long bill straight and rather slender, long legs bright yellow. In flight shows white rump and light tail but no wing bar.

Voice: A soft, one to three noted whistle (cf. Greater Yellowlegs).

Distribution: Uncommon visitor October to May. Breeds northern North America, migrates to very tip of South America.

Heads of Greater (top) and Lesser (lower) Yellowlegs

GREATER YELLOWLEGS *Totanus melanoleucus*   pl. 9

Identification: 1. 14″, b. 2″. Very similar to Lesser Yellowlegs, best separated by bill size and shape. In present species bill is long and dark, sometimes appearing slightly upturned, also bill is much longer and heavier compared to Lesser Yellowleg's which is thin and almost phalarope-like. In flight shows no wing bar but white rump and pale tail.

Voice: Call a loud two-four syllabled whistle, louder and more forceful than that of the Lesser Yellowlegs. Call is amongst best field marks, not so much number of syllables but the quality.

Distribution: Very rare visitor, mainly on the coast. Breeds North America and winters south to Cape Horn.

Greater Yellowlegs

SPOTTED SANDPIPER *Actitis macularia* pl. 10

Identification: 1. 7″, b. 0.9″. A small, 'neat-looking' wader, olive-brown above and white below. Brown of back sometimes encroaches on to sides of breast. A white line over eye. (In breeding plumage underparts are spotted black.) Short, thin beak dark with light base, feet and legs flesh-coloured. In flight shows wing bar and white sides to tail. A very active bird—constantly bobbing and dipping.

Flight: Characteristic—rather fluttery. Several quick, shallow wing beats followed by a short glide on stiff wings. In flight wings are not brought above the level of body.

Voice: Flight call 'peet-weet'.

Distribution: A regular visitor in small numbers between August and May most years. Breeds North America, migrates as far as Chile.

WANDERING TATTLER *Heteroscelus incanum* pl. 9

Identification: 1. 10″, b. 1.5″. This dark, rather featureless wader is commonest shorebird in islands. In nonbreeding plumage upperparts dark brown or grey, breast grey contrasting with white belly. In breeding plumage underparts heavily barred black. Black line from base of bill to eye and a white stripe above eye. White eye ring. Bill dark, legs yellow. In flight shows no markings on wings or tail.

Voice: Six-eight musical notes. A very quarrelsome bird.

Distribution: Very common migrant shorebird, outnumbering all the other waders in the islands. Recorded all months but in greatly reduced numbers in northern summer. Commonest on rocky shores. Breeds northern America, migrates to Pacific islands, rare on South American mainland.

Spotted Sandpiper

Wandering Tattler

WILLET *Catoptrophorus semipalmatus* pl. 9

Identification: 1. 16″, b. 2.5″. In nonbreeding plumage, this wader is a rather nondescript grey bird with a paler belly. When wings opened easily identified by flashy black, white and grey wing pattern. (In breeding plumage upper and lower parts speckled black.) In flight shows a white rump. Bill long and rather thick, legs long and grey.
Voice: Rapid 'keep-keep-keep'.
Distribution: Regular migrant in small numbers to sandy beaches; recorded all months except May and July. Breeds North America, migrates as far as northern Chile.

KNOT *Calidris canutus*

Identification: 1. 10″, b. 1.4″. A stocky, medium-sized, grey wader with short, thin, black bill and greenish legs. Upperparts grey and usually back has a scaly appearance, underparts white (red in breeding dress). In flight shows ill-defined pale rump patch and slightly darker tail, also a wing bar.
Voice: A two note whistle.
Distribution: Two records; breeds in Arctic, migrates as far as Chile.

Knot in nonbreeding plumage

LEAST SANDPIPER *Erolia minutilla* pl. 10

Identification: 1. 6″, b. 0.7″. This and the next three species are very similar and specific identification when a single species is present is often impossible. This species noticeably the smallest. Upperparts brown, usually with a few rufous feathers, pale stripe above eye, white underparts except for some streaking on breast. In all plumages the brownest of these species and has the most streaking on breast. In flight shows wing bar. Dark bill is short, slightly drooping and noticeably tapering. Legs and feet diagnostically yellow or green but beware they may be covered in mud.

Voice: 'Breep' or 'kree-eet'—more drawn out than similar notes of the Western Sandpiper.

Distribution: Regular visitor in small numbers September to May. Commoner than the succeeding three species. Breeds North America, migrates to southern Chile.

Least Sandpiper

SEMIPALMATED SANDPIPER *Ereunetes pusillus*

Identification: 1. 6.5″, b. 0.6″. Similar to Least Sandpiper but slightly larger and greyer and with a shorter, stouter bill. Legs and feet blackish. Best separated from Least by leg colour, less tapering bill and, in winter plumage, by less brown above and on breast. Separated from Western Sandpiper by shorter bill which does not droop at the tip, and call.

Voice: Single 'krip' (which lacks the 'ee' normal in the call of Least and Western) or 'cherk'.

Distribution: Few records; breeds Arctic, migrates to Chile.

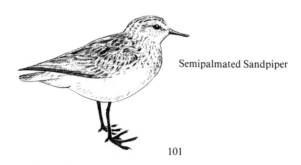

Semipalmated Sandpiper

WESTERN SANDPIPER *Ereunetes mauri* **pl. 10**

Identification: 1. 6.5″, b. 1″. Very difficult to identify but slightly larger than Semipalmated and has a longer, thicker based bill with (typically) a more drooping tip. In breeding plumage more dark rufous in upperparts than other species. Legs black.

Voice: 'Cheep', 'jeep' or 'jeep'—higher and thinner notes than those of Semipalmated and less drawn out than Least.

Distribution: Recorded in small numbers most years. Breeds Alaska and Siberia, winters south to Peru.

Western Sandpiper

BAIRD'S SANDPIPER *Erolia bairdii*

Identification: 1. 7″, b. 0.9″. Slightly larger than three previous species and identification often helped by most individuals having buffy head and breast and scaly appearance of back caused by pale edgings to feathers. Straight, slender dark bill and blackish legs. In flight wing bar is least distinct in Baird's Sandpiper.

Voice: The normal 'kreep' is fairly distinctive.

Distribution: Few records; nests in Arctic migrates to South America.

Baird's Sandpiper

WHITE-RUMPED SANDPIPER *Erolia fuscicollis*

Identification: 1. 7", b. 0.9". Similar to the previous four species but noticeably greyer in nonbreeding plumage and immediately distinguishable by the completely white rump patch (others have only the sides of rump white). Legs and feet dark. In flight pale wing bar and white rump.

Voice: Thin 'jeet'.

Distribution: Few records. Breeds in Arctic and migrates to southern South America.

PECTORAL SANDPIPER *Calidris melanotos*

Identification: 1. 8.5", b. 1.1". At rest this rather dark wader has a rather upright stance. Upperparts brown with black and white streaks. Breast buff, finely streaked brown with these markings ending abruptly at white of belly. White eye stripe. Bill relatively short and straight, mainly dark but olive at base. Legs yellowish green. In flight faint wing bar but best field mark is white sides to the rump contrasting with the dark centre.

Voice: 'Trrip-trrip' or 'prrp'.

Distribution: Recorded from the highlands of Santa Cruz (twice) and Villamil (once). Breeds in the Arctic, migrates south to Chile.

Pectoral Sandpiper

SANDERLING *Crocethia alba*   pl. 10

Identification: 1. 8″, b. 1″. By far the whitest of the small waders. In nonbreeding plumage, all-white except for very pale grey mantle, dark wing tips and characteristic black 'wrist' on bended wing. Bill and legs black. In breeding plumage head and upperparts rusty. Runs along the tide-edge like clockwork toy.

Voice: Short 'kip' or 'kit'.

Distribution: Regular migrant during northern winter and some birds oversummer. The commonest of the grey waders. Especially fond of sand beaches. An Arctic breeder which occurs on virtually the whole coastline of South America.

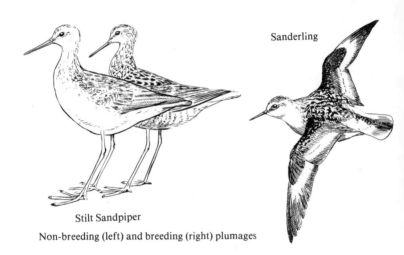

Sanderling

Stilt Sandpiper

Non-breeding (left) and breeding (right) plumages

STILT SANDPIPER *Micropalama himantopus*

Identification: 1. 8″, b. 1.6″. A grey wader, rather like Lesser Yellowlegs but with green (not yellow) legs, and a more conspicuous stripe over eye. Bill is proportionately longer and usually droops slightly at tip. Upperparts grey, underparts mainly white but some streaking on the breast. In flight shows white rump, a moderately dark tail and no wing bar. Separated from Dowitcher by rump and tail pattern and shorter bill.

Voice: A low 'querp'—rather hoarser and lower than similar note of Lesser Yellowlegs.

Distribution: Vagrant, three records October-April. Breeds in Arctic, migrant to South America.

WHIMBREL *Numenius phaeopus* **pl. 9**
Identification: 1. 17″, b. 3-4″. Unmistakable large, mottled wader with long decurved beak and long legs. Underparts slightly paler. Pale buff or white lines above eye and through crown alternate with dark stripes. In flight no markings on wing or tail. Bill brown, legs grey to black.
Voice: Call of five to seven rapid whistles is diagnostic.
Distribution: The commonest large wader in the islands, recorded all months but far less common May to July. A bird of rocky shores, lagoons and, in small numbers, the treeless highlands. Breeds in Arctic, widespread migrant.

MARBLED GODWIT *Limosa fedoa* **pl. 9**
Identification: 1. 18″, b. 4-5″. Large, rich mottled brown shorebird with long, slightly upturned bill and long legs. Spotted above, less so below. Underwings rufous. In flight no wing or tail marks. Bill dark with pinkish base, legs greenish. More buffy than Whimbrel and has up (not down) tilted bill.
Voice: 'Godwit'.
Distribution: Very rare visitor August to March. Breeds North American prairies, migrates to Pacific shores of South America.

Whimbrel

105

HUDSONIAN GODWIT *Limosa haemastica*

Identification: l. 14″, b. 3″. Similar shape to Marbled Godwit but is grey and white (winter) or red-brown (summer) with a black tail with white tip and lower rump, and whitish wing bar. Willet lacks the black tail.

Distribution: Single record. Breeds Arctic, winters in South America, usually on Atlantic coast.

SHORT-BILLED DOWITCHER *Limnodromus griseus*   pl. 9

Identification: l. 11″, b. 2.2″. The most conspicuous feature is long, snipe-like bill. Upperparts grey except for white lower back, rump and tail. Tail narrowly barred with black. Underparts greyish or white, (red in breeding plumage). Legs greenish. In flight white rump and tail make white line up back.

Voice: A whistled 'tu-tu-tu'—musical and similar to a note of the Lesser Yellowlegs.

Distribution: Rare visitor late August to May. Breeds North America, winters south to Peru.

Note: The Long-billed Dowitcher could conceivably occur but the differences from the present species (the Long-billed having a slightly longer bill, more finely barred tail and a single, thin call 'keek') are so slight as to make separation very difficult.

Short-billed Dowitcher

RECURVIROSTRIDAE: Avocets and stilts

COMMON STILT *Himantopus himantopus*   **pl.9**
Local names Tero Real, Changamé
Identification: 1. 15″, b. 2.2″. A tall, very slim wader with extremely long, red legs and thin, straight, black bill. Upperparts and wings mainly black, contrasting with white underparts and white patches behind eye and on rump. Pale brown tail. Other black and white wader is the Oystercatcher which has a stout red bill.
Flight: Legs trail far behind tail.
Voice: An extremely fussy and noisy bird—usual call 'yap-yap-yap-yap'.
Food: Invertebrates picked from water or mud.
Breeding: Solitary. Four green-brown mottled eggs laid in a scrape near water edge. All recorded nests in warmer part of year.
Distribution: Common resident on salt lagoons and fresh water pools. Species worldwide.

PHALAROPODIDAE: Phalaropes

NORTHERN (RED-NECKED) PHALAROPE   **pl. 10**
Lobipes lobatus
Identification: 1. 7″, b. 0.9″. By far the commonest phalarope in area and only wader likely to be seen resting on the sea. In winter plumage (always in our area), back blackish or dark grey with two buffy or whitish longitudinal streaks which often appear to meet on lower back. Black patch behind eye, and another on crown usually extending farther anteriorly than in Red Phalarope. Underparts white. Bill thin and black; legs and feet dark. In flight conspicuous white wing bar. On the sea phalaropes float very buoyantly and hold their necks stretched upright.
Flight: When disturbed from water fly a short distance just above the sea before turning and landing.
Voice: Sharp, rather tinkling 'whit'.
Distribution: Very common visitor to Galapagos waters between August and April. Largest numbers around the turn of the year when flocks of thousands seen between the southern and central islands and off north Isabela. Small numbers also occur on salt lagoons. Breeds in Arctic, winters at sea off western South America.

RED (GREY) PHALAROPE *Phalaropus fulicarius*   pl. 10

Identification: 1. 8″, b. 0.8″. In winter plumage pale grey or white, darker towards wing tips. Often a little streaking on back. Typical phalarope patch behind eye. Bill stouter (less needle-like, thicker at tip) than that of the Northern and yellowish with dark tip. Feet and legs horn. Crown may be white, the black of the nape often not extending far anteriorly. Appears to be lighter overall than the Northern Phalarope and wing bar less contrasting.

Voice: Sharp 'whit'.

Distribution: Few records, possibly overlooked. Breeds Arctic, winters at sea off Peru and Chile.

Wilson's Phalarope

WILSON'S PHALAROPE *Steganopus tricolor*   pl. 9

Identification: 1. 8-10″, b. 1.3″. Rather like Lesser Yellowleg but smaller and differently shaped. Upperparts pale grey except for white rump and light tail. Underparts white, sides of neck either white or (in breeding plumage) cinnamon. Needle-shaped bill dark, legs and feet green or brown. No wing bar.

Voice: Grunt.

Distribution: Regular visitor in small numbers August to December, rare other months. Usually occurs on coastal lagoons and crater lakes. Breeds North America and winters south to Chile.

STERCORARIIDAE: Skuas

SOUTHERN/SOUTH POLAR SKUA *Catharacta skua/maccormicki*

Identification: 1. 21-23", w.s. to 5'. Skuas are brown, powerfully built seabirds with conspicuous white wing flashes caused by white shafts to primaries. Much heavier than Jaegers. Bill stout, legs and feet black. Rounded end to tail.

Identification is difficult. The South Polar Skua is the more likely to occur for it is a regular migrant to the northern hemisphere. It is slightly the smaller and more delicate; light phase birds are distinguished by the sharp contrast between the light head and underparts and blackish upperparts but dark phased birds are very similar to Pomarine Jaegers but lack the tail projections. Southern Skuas are mostly larger and darker; Chilean birds are often tinged cinnamon.

Flight: Strong with rather slow, deliberate wing beats. Very fast and manoeuvrable when chasing other birds.

Distribution: One record. Breed Antarctica to southern Chile, migrate northwards.

Skua

POMARINE JAEGER (SKUA) *Stercorarius pomarinus*

Identification: 1. 22″, w.s. 4′. Large, falcon-shaped seabird with dark brown upperparts but white shafts to primaries make white flash on wing. Underparts either dark, or pale with dark band across the breast. Adult has central two tail feathers elongated, blunt tipped and twisted. Immature jaegers lack these long tail projections and are extremely difficult to identify.

Flight: When cruising quite slow and steady with slow wing beats.

Distribution: Few records within the islands but not uncommon between Galapagos and Panama. Breeds Arctic, migrates south.

Pomarine Jaeger

PARASITIC JAEGER (ARCTIC SKUA) *Stercorarius parasticus*
Stercorarius parasiticus

Identification: 1. 19″, w.s. 40″. Smaller than Pomarine but similarly coloured. Adult tail projections pointed, up to 3″ long, lacking in immature.

Distribution: Several 'probable' records, occurs at sea off Ecuador. Breeds northern North America, migrates south.

LONG-TAILED JAEGER (SKUA) *Stercorarius longicaudus*

Identification: 1. 22″ incl. 7″ tail streamers, w.s. 34″. Slender, long tail streamers of adult diagnostic, immatures lack these.

Distribution: One 'probable', occurs between Galapagos and mainland. Breeds in Arctic, migrates to South America.

LARIDAE: Gulls and terns

SWALLOW-TAILED GULL *Creagrus furcatus* **pl. 11**

Local name Gaviota blanca

Identification: 1. 20″, w.s. 45″. Only common whitish gull in area, and the only gull with a forked tail. Adult has back and wings grey and rest of body white. In breeding condition head and upper neck very dark grey forming a hood. Nonbreeding birds have dark restricted to small patch behind eye but this plumage is not often seen in the islands. A conspicuous white patch at base of bill and crimson eye-ring. Legs and feet red, bill dark with pale tip. In flight shows triangular white wing patches (page 115). Immature white, heavily spotted dark brown, with terminal black band to the tail, dark legs, bill and eye-ring.

Flight: Rather slow wing beats—similar to an egret.

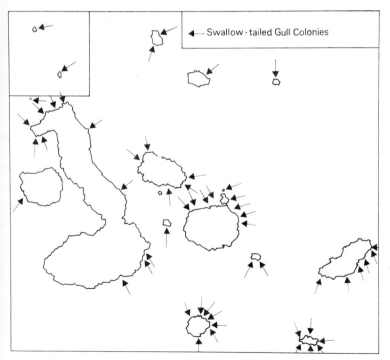

Swallow - tailed Gull Colonies

Plate 7

GROUND, CACTUS AND VEGETARIAN FINCHES

Ground Finches have male plumage black, females and immatures streaked. Beaks black in breeding plumage, pale at other times. In most cases plumages are of little use for specific identification.

Plate 8

TREE FINCHES, WARBLER FINCH AND YELLOW WARBLER

These finches are less streaked and have more green in the plumage than the Ground Finches. Males are never completely black. Beaks black in breeding plumage, pale at other times. In most cases plumages are of little use for specific identification.

1. **Small Tree Finch** *Camarhynchus parvulus*   149
   Bill short and conical

2. **Medium Tree Finch** *Camarhynchus pauper*   150
   Medium-sized beak. Only on Floreana

3. **Large Tree Finch** *Camarhynchus psittacula*   151
   Bill medium long, parrot-like

4. **Woodpecker Finch** *Camarhynchus pallidus*   152
   Bill elongated and rather stout. Extremely little streaking; no black in plumage

5. **Mangrove Finch** *Camarhynchus heliobates*   154
   Very similar to **4** but paler underparts with a little streaking; no black. Restricted range

6 **Warbler Finch** *Certhidea olivacea*   155
   Small, bill thin and pointed. Some males have orange throat

7. **Yellow Warbler** *Dendroica petechia*   129
   a, Male: bright yellow with chestnut marking on head and underparts
   b, Female: lacks chestnut markings
   c, Pale form: always some yellow somewhere—usually in wings or tail

Voice: Thin, harsh scream and a very ungull-like rattle.

Food: Fish and squid caught at night. The only nocturnal gull in the world.

Breeding: Colonial. Single buff speckled egg laid on a platform of small stones on a cliff ledge or beach. Each pair breeds every nine or ten months. The youngest breeders are aged 40 months, the survival of adults between breeding cycles is 95%, so the mean life span is 20-30 years.

Distribution: Common on small islands and cliffs of larger islands except in the colder waters off east Fernandina and west Isabela. Population 10,000-15,000 pairs. Outside the breeding times, birds migrate to the seas off Ecuador and Peru. Apart from a few pairs on Malpelo Island (Colombia), restricted to Galapagos.

SOUTHERN BLACK-BACKED (KELP) GULL
Larus dominicanus

Identification: 1. 23″, w.s. 4′. Adult white with very dark wings and mantle, bill yellow; immature mottled brown, tail brown, bill dark.

Distribution: Single bird remained for two years. Breeds widely in southern hemisphere including Peru.

Note: The superficially similar adult Band-tailed Gull *L. belcheri,* which breeds in Peru sometimes occurs north to Ecuador, has a broad black subterminal band to the tail and (winter) a heavily streaked head; immature mottled brown upper parts, whitish underparts, tail black with white tip.

LAVA GULL *Larus fuliginosus*   pl. 11
Local name Gaviota morena

Identification: 1. 21″. The only dark gull in Galapagos. Adult has body dark grey, paler under belly and base of upper tail. Head and upper neck almost black forming a hood, white eyelids. Wings almost black. Bill and legs black, inside of mouth scarlet. Immature has much brown in plumage.

Voice: Typically gull-like.

Food: Scavenges on tideline, around fishing boats and human settlements. Also a predator on seabird eggs, small fish and newly hatched marine iguanas.

Breeding: Solitary nester. Two olive, heavily blotched, eggs laid in a scrape near a lagoon, sand beach or on low rock outcrop. Nests throughout the year.

Distribution: Widely, but sparsely, distributed breeder on coasts throughout area. Total population less than 400 pairs. Endemic.

FRANKLIN'S GULL *Larus pipixcan*   pl. 11
Identification: 1. 14″. A small white gull. Adult white with grey mantle and

(in breeding plumage) black head; in nonbreeding dress the black of head restricted to patch behind eye. Wing markings important, the very tips of primaries are white, inside these is band of black separated from grey of main wing by a white band. Legs, feet and bill red. Immature, most commonly seen, wings and mantle brown, and black subterminal band on tail, giving an impression of there being a white rump patch. Hind part of the head is grey, legs pink, bill horn. For differences from Laughing Gull see that species.

Distribution: Regular migrant in very variable numbers, possibly increasing. Most birds October to May. Immatures predominate and may include some misidentified Laughing Gulls. Breeds inland in North America and migrates in large numbers as far as Chile.

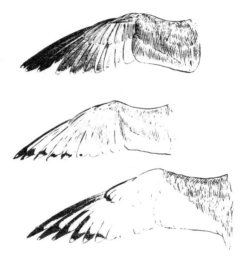

Wings of adult Laughing Gull (top), Franklin's Gull (middle)
and Swallow-tailed Gull (lower)

LAUGHING GULL *Larus atricilla*

Identification: 1. 16". Adult similar to Franklin's Gull but has uniformly dark wing tips and a slightly larger, 'drooping' bill. First year Laughing Gull is much browner on head, neck and breast than young Franklin's but other immatures indistinguishable in the field.

Distribution: Few records but far less common than Franklin's Gull; specific indentification often impossible as most birds are immature. Breeds North America (and Venezuela) and migrates south to Peru.

ROYAL TERN *Sterna maxima*   pl. 11

Identification: 1. 19″. Large, heavily built tern with grey mantle, black cap and crest but white forehead. Tail fairly deeply forked. Heavy bill orange or yellow-orange, legs and feet black.

Flight: Powerful and more gull-like than other terns in area.

Voice: An attention-drawing, shrill 'keer'.

Distribution: Regular migrant in small numbers, most common January to March at Villamil (Isabela). Nests North America, migrant as far as Peru.

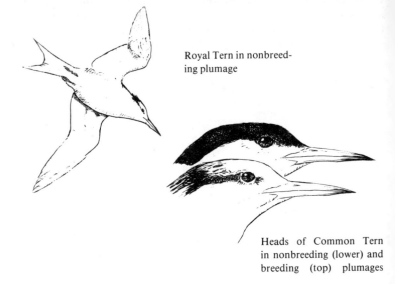

Royal Tern in nonbreed-
ing plumage

Heads of Common Tern
in nonbreeding (lower) and
breeding (top) plumages

COMMON TERN *Sterna hirundo*   pl. 11

Identification: 1. 14″. Small, rather slim, white tern with grey mantle. In nonbreeding plumage adult has incomplete black cap and white forehead; bill mainly black, sometimes with red base. (When breeding complete black cap, red bill with black tip.) Immatures like winter adults but have dusky shoulder patch.

Flight: Light and rather buoyant.

Voice: Harsh 'keer-arr'.

Distribution: Few definite records but some immatures of this species and/or Arctic Terns. *S. paradisaea* occur in most northern winters. Immatures and nonbreeding adults of these species are virtually indistinguishable.

Fairy Tern

FAIRY TERN *Gygis alba*

Identification: 1. 12″. Entirely white save for black ring around eye, black bill with blue base, dark feet and legs.
Flight: Light and erratic.
Distribution: Single record, breeds on many tropical islands.

BROWN NODDY *Anous stolidus* pl. 11

Local names Nodi, Gaviotín cabeza blanca
Identification: 1. 15″, w.s. 30″. A very dark brown tern with pointed wings and long, wedge-shaped tail. Dark colour relieved only by whitish forehead and top of head, and white eyelids. Much smaller and slimmer than all dark Lava Gull and does not sit on beaches or lagoons.
Flight: Steady and level with rather slow wing beats.
Voice: Rarely a low growl.
Food: Small fish picked from surface of sea. Often feeds in association with other seabirds and predatory fish. Accompanies feeding pelicans and will sit on head or back of these birds.
Breeding: Nests in small colonies on seacliffs and in shallow caves. A single blotched egg laid on the bare rock in any month but fewest eggs noted August to October. Pairs may lay at less than annual intervals.
Distribution: Common breeder throughout archipelago. Widespread in tropical seas.

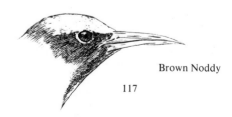

Brown Noddy

117

SOOTY TERN *Sterna fuscata*   **pl. 11**

Local name Gaviotín

Identification: 1. 16″. Only Galapagos tern with contrasting black and white plumage, and long, deeply forked tail. Adult has upperparts black except for broad white band on forehead and long, white outer-tail feathers. Underparts entirely white. Immature brown, feathers of wings and mantle tipped with white.

Flight: Very buoyant with slow and continuous wing beats. Body appears to move up and down with each beat.

Food: Small fish.

Breeding: No information.

Distribution: Breeds on Culpepper but rarely seen elsewhere in islands as birds fly north to feed in warmer waters.

Sooty Tern

BLACK TERN *Chlidonias niger*

Identification: 1. 9.5″. Upperparts grey, underparts whitish with grey patch on side of breast, most of head and upper neck blackish. Bill black. Tail slightly forked. (In summer mainly black.)

Distribution: A single dead immature. Common off the Gulf of Guayaquil. Breeds in North America, winters south to Peru.

COLUMBIDAE: Pigeons

GALAPAGOS DOVE *Zenaida galapagoensis*   **pl. 6**
Local name Paloma

Identification: 1. 8″. This small, very tame dove is the only pigeon resident in the islands. Upperparts mainly brown but wing coverts and mantle feathers black and white. Neck and breast wine red, belly slightly paler. Bronze green patch on side of neck, bright blue eye ring, red legs and feet. Immatures less brightly coloured.

Flight: Level and fast with rapid wing beats. During display the wing beats are slower and much exaggerated.

Voice: Usually silent but males have, when displaying, a very quiet, deep cooing.

Food: Seeds, caterpillars, cactus pulp and flowers if available.

Breeding: Two white eggs laid in a rough nest of grass built under a rock or in an old mockingbird nest. Nests found in all months. When nesting will attempt to lead intruders away by injury-feigning.

Distribution: Drier parts of the main islands. Commonest on Hood, Tower, Pinta, James, Barrington and inside the crater of Fernandina— places with few or no introduced cats. Endemic.

EARED DOVE *Zenaida auriculata*

Identification: 1. 10″. Olive-brown, underparts pinkish; black wing spots and cheek marks. Tail pointed and all but inner feathers tipped white or cinnamon.

Distribution: Single record. Widespread in South America.

CUCULIDAE: Cuckoos

DARK-BILLED CUCKOO *Coccyzus melacoryphus*   **pl. 6**
Local names Cuclillo, Aguatero

Identification: 1. 11″—about half of which is tail. Very secretive bird with a long dark tail, feathers with broad white tips. Upperparts grey-brown with much rufous on wings, crown grey. Underparts pale rust except for grey sides of throat. Legs and stout beak black.

Flight: Low with rapid wing beats; usually prefers to escape attention by hopping through the undergrowth.

Voice: A low chuckling. More often heard than seen.
Food: Insects, including caterpillars, moths, grasshoppers.
Breeding: Up to five green eggs laid in a nest of twigs and moss placed in tree or bush. Season January to May.
Distribution: Common only on Isabela, Floreana, Fernandina, Santa Cruz and San Cristóbal. Also recorded on Duncan (uncommon), James (possibly a recent colonist) and Barrington (once). Widespread in South America.

BLACK-BILLED CUCKOO *Coccyzus erythropthalmus*

Identification: 1. 11″. Like the resident species but has upperparts entirely brown and lacks grey on head and rufous on wings. Underparts white. Bill black.
Distribution: Single record. Breeds in North America and migrates to north Peru.

GROOVE-BILLED ANI *Crotophaga sulcirostris*   pl. 12
SMOOTH-BILLED ANI *C. ani*

Identification: 1. 12″. Very distinctive all-black, cuckoo-shaped birds with short wings and long floppy tails. Specific identifications often difficult. The Smooth-billed Ani is slightly larger with the bill strongly arched and with a high narrow ridge. The Groove-billed Ani has a similar laterally compressed bill with three grooves on the upper mandible. When perched the tail droops and flaps in the wind.
Flight: Weak and laboured.
Voice: Mourning "ouuuii" (Smooth-billed) or whistled "kuke, kuke, kuke" (Groove-billed).
Distribution: Three records of Groove-billed Ani in 1960s and a few Smooth-billed Anis seen in the farmland of Santa Cruz 1980-1. Nest in the Americas, not migratory though individuals frequently wander well outside the normal range. In view of the basically sedentary nature, the weak flight and association with cattle (from which they are credited with removing ticks), there is the possibility that these individuals .may have been brought to the islands by man.

TYTONIDAE: Barn Owls

BARN OWL *Tyto alba*   **pl. 4**

Local names Lechuza de campanarios, Lechuza blanca

Identification: 1. 10″. A very pale owl with heart-shaped facial disc. Upperparts dark brown-grey, speckled with black and white; facial disc white or buff, outlined dark. A nocturnal species, roosting by day.

Flight: Rather moth-like with deep wing beats and occasional glides.

Voice: A long 'kreeee...'; higher pitched and shriller than the note of Short-eared Owl.

Food: Mainly rats and mice, some small birds. Eats more crickets, grasshoppers and scorpions than the Short-eared Owl. Hunts by night.

Breeding: Few records of one or two white eggs laid on the floor of a cave in November-December, February and July.

Distribution: Recorded from Santa Cruz, Isabela, James, San Cristóbal and Fernandina. Scarce except on Fernandina. Cosmopolitan.

STRIGIDAE: Owls

SHORT-EARED OWL *Asio flammeus*   **pl. 4**

Local name Lechuza de campo

Identification: 1. 14″, w.s. 37″. Much darker and commoner than Barn Owl. Upperparts dark brown with some buff mottling, underparts buff with brown streaking, heaviest on breast. Circular facial disc dark, outlined with black and white. Short 'ear-tufts' often difficult to see. In flight shows black patch near bend of underwing. Bill dark, feet and legs covered with pale feathers, eye bright yellow.

Flight: Appears noticeably broad winged and flies with deep wing beats.

Voice: A dog-like yapping as a warning near nest, display call 'whoo-whoo-whoo...'. Young have a long drawn-out begging call 'skreeeep'.

Food: Wide variety of birds, rats, mice, some invertebrates. Regular visitor to seabird colonies to prey on storm petrels, shearwaters, etc. Hunts by day and night.

Breeding: Strongly territorial. Three to five white eggs laid on ground among thick vegetation or between rocks. Nests all months but most December to April.

Distribution: Recorded from all the main islands except Wenman, but only two records from Jervis and few from Fernandina. Commonly seen on smaller islands but probably does not nest in these areas. Cosmopolitan.

CAPRIMULGIDAE: Nightjars

COMMON NIGHTHAWK *Chordeiles minor* **pl. 12**
Identification: 1. 9″. A slim, brownish grey, hawk-like bird with conspicuously crooked wings and longish tail. Body entirely grey with darker markings, except for buff or white throat patch. Diagnostic white band on the wing between the bend of the wing and the wing tip. In addition the male has white band near the tip of tail.
Flight: Erratic and often changes from slow to fast wing beats. Flies quite high when disturbed by day or feeding in the evening.
Distribution: Rare visitor, breeds North and Central America and migrates south.

APODIDAE: Swifts

CHIMNEY SWIFT *Chaetura pelagica*
Identification: 1. 5″, w.s. 12″. All-black with curved wings and extremely short, slightly rounded tail.
Flight: Fast and direct, quite unlike swallows and martins.
Distribution: One record. Breeds North America, winters south to Peru.

ALCEDINIDAE: Kingfishers

BELTED KINGFISHER *Ceryle alcyon* **pl. 12**
Identification: 1. 13″. A conspicuous, noisy, large headed and large billed bird. Blue-grey above, white underneath except for single blue breast band in male, and a blue and a rufous band in female. Very pronounced crest.
Flight: Direct and fast with deep, irregular wing beats. Often hovers and then plunges into water after fish.
Distribution: An annual visitor October to March in very small numbers. Breeds North America, migrates to extreme northern parts of South America.

TYRANNIDAE: New World Flycatchers

VERMILION FLYCATCHER *Pyrocephalus rubinus*   **pl. 6**
Local name Brujo
Identification: 1. 5″. Adult male unmistakable with crown and underparts brilliant red shown off by black eyestripe, upperparts and tail. Females and young brown above, bright yellow underneath except for almost white throat and chin, a pale stripe above eye. Immature male pink underneath. Bill dark, legs and feet black.
Voice: The display flight is accompanied by a rapid 'tinka-tinka-tinka' or 'tee-tui-tui-tui-tuieet-tui' with the calls interspaced with bill snaps.
Food: Insects caught from a perch by aerial chase or picked from the ground.
Breeding: Territorial. Three eggs laid in a cup nest of moss, lichens, etc. placed high in a tree. Breeds during the warmer part of the year.
Distribution: Has been recorded on all main islands except Tower. Only single records on Hood and Wenman, now extinct on Barrington and Jervis. Although it does occur near the coast, it is a bird of the highlands. Widespread in the Americas, though elsewhere the female has white and pink, not yellow, underparts. The Galapagos race is endemic.

LARGE-BILLED FLYCATCHER *Myiarchus magnirostris*   **pl.6**
Local names Papa moscas, María
Identification: 1. 6″. Slightly larger than Vermilion Flycatcher with larger bill. Upperparts grey-brown, chin, throat and breast grey, belly sulphur-yellow but never so bright a yellow as in female Vermilion. Closed wing shows double wing bar.
Voice: Common call is a liquid 'wheet-we' or 'wheet-wheet-we'. Also a melodious song.
Breeding: Territorial. Up to four eggs laid in a nest of vegetable matter in hole in tree or cactus, or in old finch nest.
Distribution: Widespread on all the main islands except Wenman (three records), Tower (one record) and Culpepper. Endemic.

HIRUNDINIDAE: Swallows and martins

GALAPAGOS MARTIN *Progne modesta*   pl. 12
Local name Golondrina

Identification: 1. 6.5". Only resident member of group. Always completely dark with pointed wings and shallowly forked tail. Adult male glossy black, female and immature very dark brown. Only likely to be confused with the much larger male Purple Martin.

Flight: Rapid, a few quick, rather stiff wingbeats followed by a long glide. Usually seen circling high in the air or sweeping fast in front of cliffs.

Voice: In flight utters a musical twittering 'tchur-tchur'.

Food: Insects caught in flight.

Breeding: Two or three white eggs laid in a hole lined with grass and feathers. Usual site in sea or inland cliff.

Distribution: Found in small numbers throughout the archipelago except the northermost islands. Commonest in the highlands. Endemic.

Heads of Purple Martin (top) and Galapagos Martin

PURPLE MARTIN *Progne subis*   pl. 12

Identification: 1. 8". Largest hirundine in Galapagos. Male either blue-black overall or may have a little pale on belly. Female brown above, breast pale but heavily streaked dark, belly white. Wings pointed, tail slightly forked. Galapagos Martin is always all-dark and so females are distinguishable. Males, however, only told by size—a very dubious field character.

Flight: Alternates quick flaps and glides. Often glides in spirals.

Distribution: Irregular visitor in very small numbers. Most records from Hood. Breeds North America and migrates to northern South America.

BANK SWALLOW (SAND MARTIN) *Riparia riparia* **pl. 12**

Identification: 5". Brown upperparts combined with white underparts and throat separated by brown breast band are diagnostic. Tail slightly forked.
Flight: Graceful and rapid. Occasionally flicks from side to side but less so than Barn Swallow.
Distribution: Rare visitor in very small numbers. Breeds North America, migrates to Tierra del Fuego.

BARN SWALLOW *Hirundo rustica* **pl. 12**

Identification: 1. 6.5". A long-winged swallow with very deeply forked tail. Upperparts blue-black, underparts buff, throat and forehead cinnamon. Shows a band of white spots near end of spread tail.
Flight: Fast, often flicks from side to side.
Distribution: Regular visitor in very small numbers. Most birds occur during the northern winter but some birds either oversummer or, more likely, survive this long before perishing. Breeds North America, migrates south.

Barn Swallow

CLIFF SWALLOW *Petrochelidon pyrrhonota*

Identification: 1. 5". Rather similar to Barn Swallow but has a pale orange or buff rump, square tail and buff forehead.
Distribution: Three records. Breeds North America, winters South America.

MIMIDAE: Mockingbirds

GALAPAGOS MOCKINGBIRD *Nesomimus parvulus*   **pl.** ●
Local name Cucuve

Identification: 1. 10″. Any thrush-sized, streaked landbird will be a mockingbird—the species depending on the island. This is the most widespread species. Upperparts grey-brown, wing coverts and each feather of long, graduated tail having pale tips. Underparts white with some streaking on sides of breast. Pale eye stripe and neck collar, black patch behind eye. Relatively long, slightly decurved beak, feet and legs dark. Eye colour varies from island to island. Juveniles more streaked than adults.

Flight: Rapid wing beats alternating with short glides. Often glides the last few feet before landing.

Voice: Call is strident and attention drawing, song loud and melodious. Does not mimic other birds.

Food: Omnivorous.

Breeding: Territorial. Nest of twigs made in tree or cactus. Two to four green eggs are normal. Laying period October to April, double brooded. Sometimes more than two birds feed the young.

Distribution: Common on all the main islands except those with another species (i.e. Floreana, Hood, San Cristóbal). Two records on Duncan (which lacks a resident mockingbird) probably refer to this species. There are considerable differences between the various island forms of this species. Endemic.

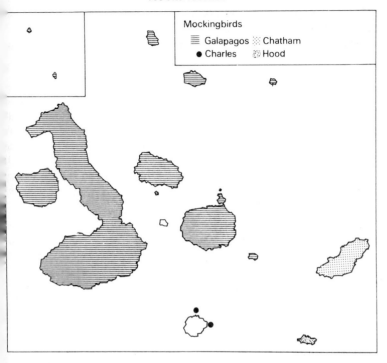

Island distribution of the four mockingbirds

CHARLES MOCKINGBIRD *Nesomimus trifasciatus*   **pl. 6**
Identification: 1. 10". Similar to the previous species but the upperparts brown with few streaks and underparts with conspicuous dark patches on the sides of the breast. Eye dark brown.
Food: Omnivorous.
Breeding: Little information but nest usually a substantial mass of twigs placed in a cactus.
Distribution: Now restricted to a total of 150 individuals on Champion and Gardner-near-Floreana. Species is not considered to be in danger of extinction. Reasons for the extinction on Floreana unknown. Endemic. Map page 127.
Note: It has been suggested that all these mockingbirds should be included in a single species. If so, it must be this species, which was the first to be described.

HOOD MOCKINGBIRD *Nesomimus macdonaldi*   **pl. 6**
Identification: 1. 11". Slightly larger than other species and has a much longer, stouter and more decurved beak. Trace of moustachial stripe and indistinct band of blotches across the breast. Tail feathers have less white than other species. Eye hazel.
Voice: More strident than other species.
Food: Omnivorous. Feeds much on carrion and seabird eggs when available, also remains of feeds given to young hawks and albatrosses.
Breeding: As other species. Single brooded in March-April; nesting often very synchronised.
Distribution: Common and endemic to Hood and Gardner-near-Hood. Map page 127.

CHATHAM MOCKINGBIRD *Nesomimus melanotis*   **pl. 6**
Identification: 10". Intermediate between Galapagos and Hood species. Some spots on the breast and a dark line on each side of the throat. Eye yellow.
Distribution: Common and endemic to San Cristóbal. Map page 127.

PARULIDAE: New World Warblers

YELLOW WARBLER *Dendroica petechia* **pl. 8**

Local name Canario

Identification: 5″. The only bright yellow bird in Galapagos. Adult has crown and entire underparts bright yellow, upperparts greenish olive, brightest on rump. Tail and wings brown with some yellow markings. Adult male has bright chestnut on crown and chestnut streaking on breast. Immature greyer, sometimes with almost white underparts but always some trace of yellow to be found, if only on the wings or tail. Warbler Finch never has any yellow in the plumage. Bill thin and pointed.

Voice: Song is a rapid series of sweet notes—'wee-chee-wee-chee-chee-ur', the ending slurred downwards.

Food: Insects caught in trees and bushes, on the ground and by flycatcher-like hawking. Often feeds in inter-tidal zone. Much noisy bill-snapping when feeding. Enters houses to catch insects.

Breeding: Territorial throughout year. Cup-shaped nest of moss and other vegetable matter placed in the canopy of tree or bush. Two or three buff spotted eggs laid December to April.

Distribution: Occurs on all main and most smaller islands, from shore to mountain top. More tied to green vegetation than is the Warbler Finch, commonest in coastal areas. Widespread from Alaska to Peru. The race in Galapagos is very similar to that in coastal Ecuador.

Yellow Warbler. Life-size

BLACKPOLL WARBLER *Dendroica striata*

Identification: 1. 5″. In winter olive-green above, two wing bars, dingy yellow underneath with slight streaks. Summer male striped with black cap. Care is needed with vagrant warblers as several species could occur.

Distribution: One record. Breeds North America, winters South America, usually east of the Andes.

THRAUPIDAE: Tanagers

SUMMER TANAGER *Piranga rubra*

Identification: 1. 7″. Adult male entirely red but other plumages grey-olive above, yellow underneath. No wing bar or black on wings as in some other North American tangers. Bill relatively long and stout, pale.

Voice: A loud, sharp 'pi-tuck'.

Distribution: Two definite records and two other unidentified tanagers. Breeds North America, migrates to Ecuador and Peru.

Summer Tanager

ICTERIDAE: American orioles and blackbirds

BOBOLINK *Dolichonyx oryzivorus* **pl. 12**

Identification: 7″. First impression is large sparrow-like bird, perhaps mistaken for an overgrown Darwin's Finch. Upperparts rich buff, with dark and pale stripings on head, underparts buff with few streaks. Each tail feather pointed. Male in breeding plumage mainly black with yellowish nape, white on rump and back. Bill conical and rather pointed.

Voice: Distinctive 'pink'.

Distribution: Regular visitor in variable numbers, commonest October to December. Normally seen in cultivated and cattle-rearing areas. Breeds North America and migrates as far as Chile.

DARWIN'S FINCHES

Few groups of such inconspicuous birds have excited such attention and given such insights into the ways, whys and wherefores of evolution as Darwin's Finches. And unlike so many of the most interesting birds, many species are not rare but are the most widespread and numerous species of birds on the islands.

The first specimens were collected by Darwin during his voyage in the islands and were described by the eminent artist and zoologist Gould. For many years the group was thought to be restricted to Galapagos but in 1891 another species was found to inhabit Cocos Island (425 miles to the north-east of the Galapagos). Therefore the term Galapagos Finches is best not used for the group.

In view of the importance of the group and the great similarities between many of the species, a general account is given before a detailed species-by-species account. Details of the flight and breeding of all species are so similar that to prevent repetition these topics are omitted from the species accounts.

TAXONOMY

After almost a hundred years of dispute and the description of many island populations as separate species, it is now agreed that there are 13 species in the Galapagos, belonging to probably four genera. Anyone interested in the evolution of the taxonomy of the group can best be directed to the excellent accounts by Swarth and Lack (whose book *Darwin's Finches* is now a classic). Sufficient here to say that Gould did an excellent job and even got the Warbler Finch into its correct position, though Darwin expressed his doubts. Later taxonomists found many minor inter-island differences which they used as bases for describing new species. The Warbler Finch was tossed around for some time before finding its way back into the finches where it undoubtedly belongs. A hypothetical family tree for the group is shown p. 138 but it must be stressed that the ancestor of the group is unknown and need not have been a finch. There is little reason why the finch-types could not have evolved from a warbler-like ancestor. The Cocos Finch is very similar to the melanic phase of the Bananaquit *Coereba flaveola,* a very widespread member of the honey-creepers, and the males would be virtually indistinguishable if they occurred together. However, these similarities might have come about by

131

Plate 9

LARGE WADERS

All in nonbreeding plumage

1. **Whimbrel** *Numenius phaeopus* 105
   Brown. Long decurved beak

2. **Oystercatcher** *Haematopus palliatus* 90
   Black and white. Red bill relatively long

3. **Marbled Godwit** *Limosa fedoa* 105
   Brown. Long upturned bill

4. **Common Stilt** *Himantopus himantopus* 107
   Black and white. Very long, thin red legs, thin black bill

5. **Solitary Sandpiper** *Tringa solitaria* 95
   Dark back, white eye-ring. In flight no rump or wing patches

6. **Willet** *Catoptrophorus semipalmatus* 100
   Pale grey; flashy black, white and grey wing markings

7. **Greater Yellowlegs** *Totanus melanoleucus* 98
   Grey; yellow legs. Bill long and dark; may appear slightly up-
   tilted

8. **Lesser Yellowlegs** *Totanus flavipes* 98
   Grey; yellow legs. Bill shorter and thinner than **7**. Commoner
   than **7**

9. **Short-billed Dowitcher** *Limnodromus griseus* 106
   Grey. Snipe-like bill

10. **Wandering Tattler** *Heteroscelus incanum* 99
    Grey; rather featureless with no wing or tail marks; yellow
    legs

11. **Wilson's Phalarope** *Steganopus tricolor* 108
    Grey and white; green legs. Dark, needle-shaped bill.
    Normally seen swimming

Plate 10

SMALL WADERS

All in nonbreeding plumage

1. **Semipalmated Plover** *Charadrius semipalmatus*   92
   Brown and white; white forehead and collar; dark breast band

2. **Black-bellied Plover** *Squatarola squatarola*   91
   Grey; legs black. Short, stout bill

3. **Ruddy Turnstone** *Arenaria interpres*   93
   Rusty or grey back. Bill dark, stout and slightly upturned. In
   flight harlequin pattern

4. **Surfbird** *Aphriza virgata*   94
   Grey and white; bill yellow with black tip; legs yellow

5. **Spotted Sandpiper** *Actitis macularia*   99
   Brown and white; white line over eye; thin beak dark with
   light base. Constantly bobs

6. **Sanderling** *Crocethia alba*   104
   Very pale grey; black wrist mark, bill and legs. Like clockwork
   toy

7. **Least Sandpiper** *Erolia minutilla*   100
   Grey-brown; streaks on breast; legs yellow or green

8. **Western Sandpiper** *Ereunetes mauri*   102
   Grey-brown. Bill with rather a thick base and (typically) a
   slightly drooping tip

9. **Red Phalarope** *Phalaropus fulicarius*   108
   Pale grey. Bill yellow with dark tip, black of nape often
   restricted

10. **Northern Phalarope** *Lobipes lobatus*   107
    Pale grey. Bill thin and black; black may extend on to crown

convergent evolution and not by any direct evolutionary connection. For the present there is no reason not to retain the original name of finch.

IDENTIFICATION

All are sparrow-sized or slightly smaller, grey, brown, black or slightly greenish birds with conspicuously short and rounded wings, short tails strong legs and feet. Many species are superficially similar if not identical in plumage and are therefore extremely confusing on first sight. However, if attention is focused on the bill, most individuals can be identified after a little experience. Some few birds are impossible to identify with any certainty—important evidence suggesting that these species arose by evolution from a common ancestor. Beginners with the group should not despair, but rather ignore any very confusing individuals. Although not truly playing the game, it helps to know which island you are on and what species occur on that island, as this helps to remove some of the more difficult options.

In most species there are sexual differences in the plumages. In the Ground and Cactus Finches the ultimate male plumage is all black except for white or buff tips on the undertail coverts, whereas all females (except Large Cactus Finch) and immatures are drab grey-brown. The attainment of the full adult plumage is related to age; some species change from immature to all black in one moult whereas most species need several years or never attain it. Male Tree and Vegetarian Finches never become completely black and most have only black head and neck. Woodpecker, Mangrove and Warbler Finches never have any black in the plumage.

As stressed above the all-important points in identification are the shape and proportions of the bill, and its size relative to the head. Bill colour is of no use as all species have the bill black when in breeding condition, and pale horn or even yellow at other times.

Care must be taken in case of freak or diseased individuals, the latter being quite frequent. Several presumed hybrids are known; Warbler Finch × a tree finch (from Floreana and San Cristóbal), Cactus × Large Cactus Finches (Pinta), Cactus Finch × Small and/or Medium Ground Finch (Santa Cruz, Plaza), Large Ground Finch × Large Cactus Finch (Tower), Woodpecker Finch × Warbler Finch (Santa Cruz), Large Cactus Finch × Sharp-beaked Ground Finch (Tower, Wenman).

FLIGHT

As with landbirds on several oceanic islands, these finches have the powers of flight somewhat reduced, presumably due to the relative freedom from predators (though they are eaten by owls and the Hawk) and the high risk of being blown out to sea and lost if they fly high or venture too far afield.

In flight all the finches constantly flap their conspicuously short and rounded wings.

VOICE

The call notes are simple and generalised. Attempts have been made to render the commoner and more distinctive of the songs but the range of variation within any one population is greater than the differences between species. Also there are considerable inter-island differences in song. Apart from a few species, e.g. Large Ground Finch, only very experienced observers can identify Darwin's Finches by song—and then often more to their own satisfaction than to their friends'.

FOOD

There is convincing evidence from the studies by Bowman and others that the beaks of different species are adapted to cope efficiently with different foods. The large bills of the ground finches are ideal for coping with seeds, the thin pointed beak of the Warbler Finch for picking insects from leaves, and so on.

BREEDING

Breeding behaviour is remarkably uniform throughout the group. All species are territorial, though the density of nests may be very high, e.g. 25 nesting pairs have been found in an area 100 yards by 25 yards.

Once conditions become suitable for breeding, often after the first rain following a drought, the male takes up a territory, builds several of the characteristic dome-shaped nests with a side entrance, and then displays at any female. In an effort to attract her he may even display at a nest of another species. After pair formation the female will either select one of the rather rough display nests for lining, or the pair may build yet another nest.

The nest is made of twigs, grass and pieces of bark, augmented and lined with lichen, hair, feathers, cottonheads as available. In size the nest varies from that of a clenched fist (Warbler Finch) to a small football (ground finches). The normal nest-site is in a bush or tree or, in cactus and ground finches, between two cactus pads. The height above the ground varies from a few inches (where the vegetation is very low) to the terminal branches of trees (especially the tree finches).

Before laying the female is fed by the male, who also supplies all her food during incubation. The average clutch is four pale eggs, speckled with brown, but two, three and five are not uncommon. Incubation, by the female alone, takes about 12 days. The young are fed in the nest for 13-14 days on soft foods, especially insect larvae and berries. Both sexes feed the young when they are in the nest but after fledging normally only the male pays them any attention. If conditions allow, there may be several broods in a season. In captivity these birds have been known to breed continuously for several months.

The timing of breeding is extremely variable and, at least in coastal areas, is dependent on the rains. On the coast breeding normally occurs December-April but in very wet seasons may be prolonged until the end of the year.

In most species of birds, breeding and moult of the wing feathers do not occur at the same time, probably because birds must be at their most efficient when feeding themselves and their young. At least in temperate birds, the feathers of the wings and tail are replaced at the end of the breeding season. Darwin's Finches moult at any time of year but the moult is immediately arrested if conditions become favourable for breeding, an adaption to living in an unpredictable environment.

DISTRIBUTION

Although the data on the island distributions are relatively complete, they are misleading for field purposes. This is due to the great fluctuations which occur in many populations, especially those in the drier areas and islands. A species may be common on an island at the end of a long rainy season and rare a few months later. Such cases have been witnessed in the Medium Ground Finch on Barrington and the Large Cactus Finch on Tower. In a few instances a finch has become extinct on an island within recorded time, e.g. Sharp-beaked Ground Finch on Santa Cruz. In a few cases there may be significant gaps in our knowledge. There is only one specimen of the Large Tree Finch from San Cristóbal and a single Sharp-beaked Ground Finch on Isabela. It seems unlikely that these two islands

Distribution of Darwin's Finches

	Santa Cruz	Plaza	Barrington	San Cristóbal	Hood	Floreana	Isabela	Fernandina	James	Jervis	Duncan	Tower	Marchena	Pinta	Wenman	Culpepper
Small Ground Finch	•	•	•	•	•	•	•	•	•	•	•		•	•		
Medium Ground Finch	•	•	•	•		•	•	•	•	•	•		•	•		
Large Ground Finch	•					•	•	•	•	•	•	•	•	•	•	
Sharp-beaked Ground Finch							•	•				•		•	•	•
Cactus Finch	•	•	•	•		•	•		•	•			•	•		
Large Cactus Finch					•							•			•	•
Vegetarian Finch	•			•		•	•	•	•	•			•	•		
Small Tree Finch	•		•	•		•	•	•	•	•	•			•		
Medium Tree Finch						•										
Large Tree Finch	•					•	•	•	•	•			•	•		
Woodpecker Finch	•			•			•	?	•		•					
Mangrove Finch							•	•								
Warbler Finch	•		•	•	•	•	•	•	•	•	•	•	•	•	•	•

Note: see the text for extra-limital and dubious records

could not support or have supported the appropriate species so more field work is obviously needed.

Aside from these inter-island differences, there are marked zonal differences on the larger, higher islands. The ground and cactus finches are commonest in the arid areas whereas tree finches and the Warbler Finch occur largely higher up. This zonation can, however, be drastically upset by extremely dry or wet periods.

CAUTION

It is only a very wise man or a fool who thinks that he is able to identify all the finches which he sees. Great caution must be observed in identifying species outside their normal ranges. Straggling from island to island certainly takes place but this is probably on a very small scale, perhaps far less than the incidence of freak individuals or hybrids.

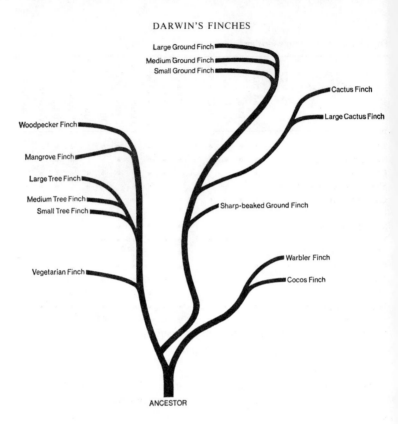

DARWIN'S FINCHES

Large Ground Finch
Medium Ground Finch
Small Ground Finch

Cactus Finch

Large Cactus Finch

Woodpecker Finch

Mangrove Finch

Large Tree Finch

Medium Tree Finch
Small Tree Finch

Sharp-beaked Ground Finch

Warbler Finch

Cocos Finch

Vegetarian Finch

ANCESTOR

Finch family tree. From Lack's
Darwin's Finches

FRINGILLIDAE: Finches

SMALL GROUND FINCH *Geospiza fuliginosa* **pl. 7**
Local name (for finch) Pinzón

Identification: 4.5″. Much the smallest and dumpiest-looking of the sparrow-like ground finches. Adult male all black except for white or buff tips to undertail coverts. Several intermediate plumages between the female-type immature and the adult male. Female and immature have feathers of upperparts dark grey, edged paler, and underparts grey with dark streaks, most noticeable on throat and breast.

Bill is sparrow-like but disproportionately smaller than in Medium and Large Ground Finches. Upper edge of beak obviously curved whereas it is almost straight in the Sharp-beaked Ground Finch (but geographical separation is often the best field identification point).

Voice: Commonest calls disyllabic 'twchoo-twchoo' or 'teur-wee'. Song is weaker than the other ground finches.

Food: Large variety of soft seeds picked from plants or from the ground; some flowers and fruit when available. Probably eats more insects than the Medium Ground Finch. Sometimes feeds on the shore. Removes ticks from tortoises, land and marine iguanas.

Distribution: Common on all main islands except Culpepper, Tower and Wenman (six recorded in 1906), where probably missing due to competition with the Sharp-beaked Ground Finch. Commonest in the arid zone but flocks occur up to the top of the volcanoes. Overall the commonest landbird. Endemic.

Small Ground Finch. Life-size

Plate 11

GULLS AND TERNS

Plate 12

HIRUNDINES AND RARE MIGRANTS

1. **Galapagos Martin** *Progne modesta* 124
   Small, all-dark

2. **Purple Martin** *Progne subis* 124
   Medium-sized; male all dark, female with streaked underparts

3. **Barn Swallow** *Hirundo rustica* 125
   Blue-black upperparts, buff and cinnamon underparts. Deeply
   forked tail

4. **Bank Swallow** *Riparia riparia* 125
   Brown back and chest band

5. **Belted Kingfisher** *Ceryle alcyon* 122
   Large head and bill. One (male) or two (female) breast bands

6. **Groove-billed Ani** *Crotophaga sulcirostris* 120
   All-black. Long, floppy tail

7. **Bobolink** *Dolichonyx oryzivorus* 130
   Streaked brown and buff. Bill conical and pointed. Each tail
   feather pointed

8. **Common Nighthawk** *Chordeiles minor* 122
   Grey; white band on wing and (male) tail

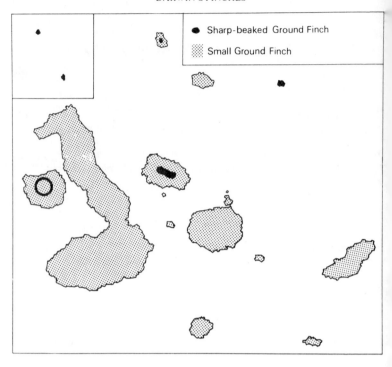

Island distribution of Sharp-beaked and Small Ground Finches

MEDIUM GROUND FINCH *Geospiza fortis* pl. 7

Identification: 1. 5". Intermediate in size between the Small and Large Ground Finches but identical in plumage. Identification only possible by beak size, but is further confused as the beak size is very variable in this species. However, the bill is never so small or pointed as Small Ground Finch. The upper edge of beak is usually much longer than the overall depth, *contra* Large Ground Finch. Despite these difficulties a little experience is sufficient to enable identification of all but the largest beaked individuals.

Voice: Louder than Small Ground Finch and also has some trisyllabic notes as 'teur-wee-we' and 'te-er-loo'.

Food: Moderately hard seeds taken from ground or plant. Few insects and larvae.

Distribution: Widespread on all the main islands except Culpepper, Tower, and Wenman (single in 1906). The few old records from Hood may refer to a now extinct population. Commonest in arid areas where often forms mixed flocks with Small Ground Finch. Also occurs, but does not breed, in the highlands. Endemic.

Remarks: Some birds on Daphne and Crossman Islands are intermediate between this species and the Small Ground Finch.

Medium Ground Finch. Small beaked and large beaked individuals from the same island. Life-size

LARGE GROUND FINCH *Geospiza magnirostris*   **pl. 7**

Identification: 1. 6.5″. By far the largest of the ground finches. Plumages identical with Small and Medium Ground Finch but a more massive beak, the depth at the base being about the same as the length. On Santa Cruz it is impossible to separate this and the very largest billed individuals of Medium Ground Finch. Any large billed ground finch feeding in a flock will be the Medium species, as the Large Ground Finch is normally solitary.

Voice: Song is a distinctive 'teu . . . e . . . e . . . leur' or 'tu-whoo-whu', slower and lower pitched than the other finches.

Food: Mainly hard seeds, rarely large insects. Feeds less on the ground than other ground finches.

Distribution: Has occurred on all the main islands except San Cristóbal, Culpepper and Hood. Possibly extinct on Floreana, and probably so on Barrington (if indeed it was ever resident there). Tends to be uncommon on islands with Medium Ground Finch. A bird of the arid zone. Endemic.

Large Ground Finch. Life-size

SHARP-BEAKED GROUND FINCH *Geospiza difficilis*   **pl. 7**

Identification: 1. 5″. Very similar to the Small Ground Finch though immature plumage is slightly darker.

The beak is rather similar to Small Ground Finch but is slightly longer and more pointed, with the upper edge almost straight. If there is any doubt as to an identification, the individual will probably be a Small Ground Finch. The beak is much smaller than that of the Cactus Finch.

Voice: Rather feeble with short notes. Song somewhat like Warbler Finch.

Food: Seeds and some insects, also flowers. Feeds mostly on the ground. On Wenman pecks at the growing wing and tail feathers of moulting boobies and drinks the blood.

Distribution: Occurs in the humid zone on James, Fernandina and Pinta, previously in similar areas on Santa Cruz but now extinct. Common on the more arid islands of Culpepper, Wenman and Tower. Single specimen from Isabela; status on San Cristóbal and Floreana doubtful but almost certainly extinct if ever resident. Endemic. Map page 142.

Sharp-beaked Ground Finch. Life-size

CACTUS FINCH *Geospiza scandens* pl. 7

Identification: 1. 5.5″. Similar to the ground finches but the female is more heavily streaked anteriorly, giving a dark area around the head and neck.

The bill, though still relatively thick, is elongated and very slightly decurved. Unlikely to be confused with other finches.

Voice: Commonest call is a ringing 'teu-lee, teu-lee'. Also a wide range of notes as 'teur-teur-teur' followed by a rapid 'twee'. Sings more in flight than the other species.

Food: Moderately hard seeds. Especially fond of the seeds, fruit, nectar and pulp of the prickly pear cactus.

Distribution: Common in the drier areas of all the main islands except Fernandina, and replaced by the Large Cactus Finch on Culpepper, Wenman, Tower and Hood; extinct on Duncan. A bird of the cactus forests—uncommon away from cacti. Always nests in an *Opuntia* (Prickly Pear Cactus). Endemic. Map page 146.

Cactus Finch. Life-size

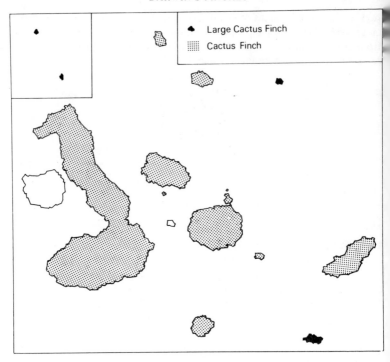

Island distribution of cactus finches

LARGE CACTUS FINCH *Geospiza conirostris* pl. 7

Identification: 1. 6''. Adult male all black except for white tips to undertail coverts. Female and immature usually dull black, on Tower rarely grey, with feathers of belly having white edgings.

Two distinctive subspecies. Birds from Hood have very heavy bills, rather similar to the Large Ground Finch but slightly more elongated and laterally compressed. Birds from northern islands are slightly smaller and have relatively smaller and narrow beaks.

Voice: Characteristic 'tlee-oo' or 'chee-you-oo'.

Food: Seeds of various sorts, large insects. On Hood digs into gravel and moves small stones to get seeds. Feeds more on open ground than Cactus Finch and not restricted to cactus areas.

Distribution: Breeds on Hood, Tower, Culpepper and Wenman; single specimens from Pinta and Gardner-near-Floreana. The two cactus finches are not found on any one island, suggesting that they have similar ecological requirements. Endemic.

Large Cactus Finches from Hood
(left) and Tower (right). Life-size

VEGETARIAN FINCH *Platyspiza crassirostris*   **pl. 7**

Identification: 1. 6.5″. One of the largest and most distinctively plumaged finches. Fully adult male has head, neck, breast, back and sides, wings and tail all black with pale or yellowish belly. However, commonest adult male plumage has head and neck black contrasting with pale underparts. Female brown above with rump olive with no streaking, underparts whitish or yellow with dark streaking on breast and sides. When perched has rather upright stance.

Bill noticeably short, deep and broad, the upper surface very convex.

Voice: Distinctive, several loud, musical notes running into a harsh churring.

Food: Soft seeds, fruits and leaves. Normally feeds quietly in bushes.

Distribution: The main islands except Barrington, Baltra, Seymour, Culpepper, Wenman, Tower and Hood, all of which are too dry to support a vegetarian species. Few old records from Duncan. Commonest in transitional zone but smaller numbers occur in both arid and humid zones. Endemic.

Vegetarian Finch. Life-size

SMALL TREE FINCH *Camarhynchus parvulus* pl. 8

Identification: 1. 4.5″. Much the smallest tree finch. Tree finches are much greener or more olive than ground finches and have few streaks. Ultimate male plumage has head, neck, breast and part of the back black, rest of upperparts grey, underparts yellowish. Many males have only head and neck black. Females are grey brown with the suggestion of pale eye-ring and stripe behind eye, underparts white or yellowish.

Bill is relatively small and conical, giving the bird a stubby appearance.

Voice: Extremely variable from a quiet, musical song to a series of rapidly repeated harsh notes. Occasional churrs and drawn out 'sees' are sometimes added to the song or used alone but such notes are more characteristic of the other tree finches.

Food: Small insects, fruits and soft seeds. Often forages on the end of the smallest branches and hangs upsidedown like a tit or chickadee. Though tree finches only rarely feed on the ground, this species does so more than the others.

Distribution: On all the main islands except Culpepper, Tower, Hood, Marchena and Wenman (two records in 1906). Commonest in the humid and transition zones but also in small numbers in the arid zone. Endemic.

Small Tree Finch. Life-size

MEDIUM TREE FINCH *Camarhynchus pauper*   **pl. 8**

Identification: 1. 5″. Adult male has head, neck and upper breast black, rest of upperparts green-olive, underparts white or yellow. Female has upperparts green-olive, underparts white or yellowish.

Bill is larger than Small Tree Finch, and smaller and less parrot-like than Large Tree Finch.

Voice: Often five-syllabic 'tju-tju-tju-tju-tju', also 'dzi-dzi-dzi'.

Food: Insects and soft seeds often picked from fruit heads.

Distribution: Endemic to Floreana where common in the highlands and uncommon or rare on the coast.

Medium Tree Finch. Life-size

LARGE TREE FINCH *Camarhynchus psittacula* **pl. 8**

Identification: 1. 5″. Larger than the other tree finches. Fully adult male has head, neck, breast and part of back black, rest of upperparts grey-brown, underparts white sometimes tinged yellow. Commoner male plumage has black restricted to head and throat giving a masked appearance. Female grey-brown above with underparts white or yellowish.

Beak is medium long and stout, upper surface curving sharply downwards and lower surface upwards, resulting in a parrot-like appearance. Bill of Woodpecker Finch is longer and straighter.

Voice: Soft and low, sometimes a bell-like note 'turelu, turelu' or 'tui-tui, tui-tui', often followed by a high pitched 'e-e-e-e-'.

Food: Largish insects and larvae, often obtained by breaking up soft plants and twigs by a twisting action of the bill.

Distribution: Recorded on all the main islands except Culpepper, Wenman, Tower and Hood. Status uncertain on San Cristóbal (old specimen, recent sight records) and probably does not breed on Barrington. Possibly extinct on Duncan. A bird of the damper areas, rarely seen on the coast. Endemic.

Large Tree Finch. Life-size

WOODPECKER FINCH *Camarhynchus pallidus* **pl. 8**

Identification: 1. 6". The largest of the light-coloured finches. Sexes similar, upperparts olive or brown with little streaking, underparts whitish or yellow with slight streaking on upper breast.

Bill tanager-like, elongated and relatively stout. Beak of Large Tree Finch is much deeper and parrot-shaped.

Voice: Song is rapid and loud. Seven or eight notes, often followed by a long drawn out 'seee'. Also notes like 'chir-kee-e-e-e', 'tchur-tchur-tchur-e-e-e-e'.

Food: Largish insects from behind bark and from soft, decaying wood, some fruit. Normal feeding is by probing into dead wood, cracks in bark or by flaking off bark. Some individuals use a twig or cactus spine for extracting otherwise unobtainable prey.

Distribution: Recorded from Santa Cruz, Isabela, San Cristóbal, Fernandina, James, Duncan (rare), Jervis (two specimens), Floreana (one specimen, few sight records), Barrington (two sight records), Pinta (one sight record). Commonest in higher zones but occurs and breeds in arid areas as well. Endemic.

Woodpecker Finch. Life-size

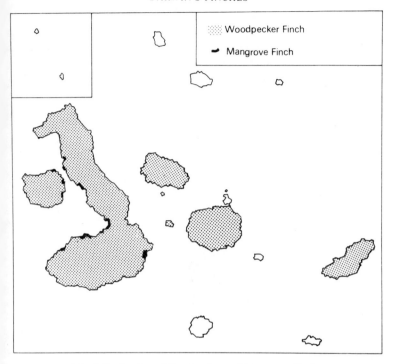

Island distribution of Woodpecker and Mangrove Finches

MANGROVE FINCH *Camarhynchus heliobates*   **pl. 8**

Identification: 1. 5.5″. Male and female similar. Upperparts brown, slightly olive on the rump, underparts white with some spotting on breast. Overall more slaty-coloured than yellow-tinged Woodpecker Finch.

Bill like Woodpecker Finch but not quite so heavy.

Voice: Song is a loud 'dschedde' repeated up to three times. May end with a rapidly rising or drawn-out 'seee'.

Food: Insects, spiders and some vegetable matter (mangrove leaves). Sometimes uses a twig to poke out insects.

Distribution: Restricted to the dense mangrove swamps on eastern Fernandina (though not seen Punta Espinosa in recent years), the coasts of western Isabela between Caleta Black to just east of Punta Moreno, and south-east Isabela, opposite the Crossman Islands. The total population must be very small due to restricted habitat. Endemic. Map page 153.

Mangrove Finch. Life-size

WARBLER FINCH *Certhidea olivacea* **pl. 8**

Local name Pinzón cantor

Identification: 1. 4". By far the smallest finch and not easily recognisable as one. Upperparts vary from olive-green to very pale grey, underparts pale buff to white. Some adult males on some islands (James, Isabela) have an orange throat patch.

The bill thin, pointed and warbler-like.

Yellow Warbler is larger and always has some trace of yellow in plumage.

Voice: Melodious song, often ending in a high-pitched buzz.

Food: Insects and spiders picked from leaves and twigs.

Distribution: Common on all main islands. Prefers the humid zone where one exists but is also common on dry islands such as Hood and Tower. Numbers vary greatly in coastal areas, e.g. usually rare at Academy Bay (Santa Cruz) but occasionally becomes common.

Warbler Finch. Life-size

Bibliography

The following titles are reviews dealing with Galapagos birds.

Bowman, R. I. 1961. Morphological differentiation and adaptation in the Galapagos finches. University of California Publications in Zoology No. 58.

Harris, M. P. 1969. Breeding seasons of sea-birds in the Galapagos Islands. Journal of Zoology (London) 159: 145-165.

Harris, M. P. 1973. The Galapagos Avifauna. Condor 75: 265-278.

Harris, M. P. 1977. Comparative ecology of seabirds in the Galapagos Archipelago, in Evolutionary Ecology (eds. Stonehouse, B. and Perrins, C.), Macmillan.

Lack, D. 1947. Darwin's Finches. Cambridge University Press.

Lack, D. 1969. Subspecies and sympatry in Darwin's Finches. Evolution 23: 252-263.

Lévêque, R. 1963. Le Statut actuel des vertebres rares et menances de l'Archipel des Galapagos. Terre et Vie 4: 397-430.

Nelson, J. B. 1968. Galapagos, island of birds. Longmans.

Swarth, H. S. 1931. The avifauna of the Galapagos Islands. Occasional papers of the California Academy of Science, No. 18.

During the last 20 years many papers on Galapagos birds have appeared in the ornithological journals of Europe and the United States of America. Most will be found under the names of I. J. and L. K. Abbott, M. Abs, P. D. Boersma, R. I. Bowman, A. Brosset, E. Curio, J. F. Downhower, D. Goodman, B. R. and P. R. Grant, J. P. Hailman, M. P. Harris, P. Kramer, R. Lévêque, J. B. Nelson, D. M. Power, J. N. M. Smith, B. K. and D. W. Snow, T. de Vries.

Index

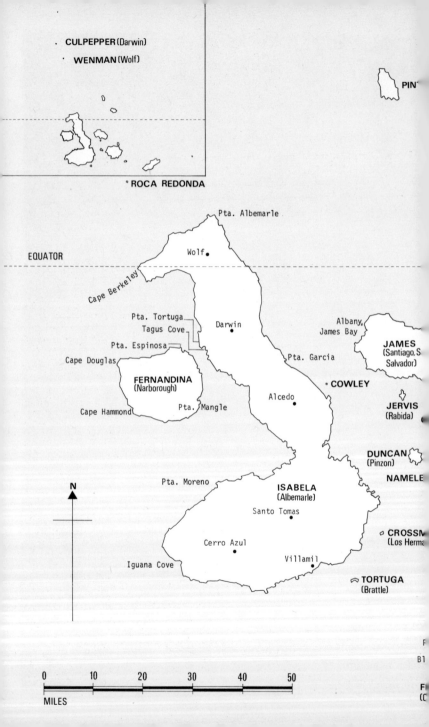